LIVING *THE SECRET* EVERYDAY

MY SECRET WORKBOOK

JOANNE SCAGLIONE
SUZANNE STITZ

❀ **Airicaly Press**
Los Angeles / New York
2007

ISBN: 1-4196-7460-9
ISBN-13: 978-1419674600

Visit www.booksurge.com to order additional copies.
www.livingthesecreteveryday.com

ALSO BY JOANNE SCAGLIONE

The Big Squeal (2005)

Life's Little Lessons (2006)

Bully-Proofing Children (2006)

To our darling daughters, Alison and Arrica
- our source of love and inspiration

*May the doors to your life open as
you open the doors to your mind.*

Joanne Scaglione
Suzanne Stitz

CONTENTS

CONTENTS

INTRODUCTION

It has been passed down through the ages, highly coveted, hidden, lost, stolen, and bought for vast sums of money. This century-old secret has been understood by some of the most prominent people in history: Plato, Galileo, Beethoven, Carnegie, Einstein– along with other inventors, theologians, scientists and great thinkers.

– Rhonda Byrne

The Secret powerfully presents the principles of the most important law of the universe: The Law of Attraction…the knowledge and use of which can transform one's life. The message of *The Secret* has been touted for years and years by many famous teachers and philosophers. But never before has there been a book devoted to making the Law of Attraction a working part of your life. *Now* comes *Living the Secret Everyday: My Secret Workbook*, adding that new dimension as it blends the ideas presented within *The Secret* along with specific applications, techniques, and recipes that will enable you to live that life you want everyday.

THE MAKING OF MY SECRET WORKBOOK

Already inspired by the notion of the Law of Attraction, we, the authors, read *The Secret* and were immediately attracted to the ideas it presented, as were millions of other people, judging by the record-breaking sales of the book. Within months of its release, *The Secret* climbed to number one on best-seller lists.

Why were so many people drawn to it? Here was a book advocating a simple philosophy that's been around for at least a hundred years, which promised to lead its followers down the road to a fulfilling life; a path to a life of being, doing, and having all that you want. The fact that you were described as the creator of your own reality and responsible for your own life struck a cord. According to *The Secret,* all you have to do is utilize your power of thought. Change your way of thinking to embrace positive thoughts and the Law of Attraction will bring more of the same. Wow, this sounded great!

But although my sister and I were totally convinced of its truth, the implementation was a bit challenging. We believed it, and we wanted to live it, but question after question surfaced as to exactly *how* to apply these wonderful ideas to our own personal experiences. We asked ourselves:

> How do I get started?
> How do I embrace it into my life on a daily basis?
> What do I really want?
> How do I change the way I've been thinking for so
> many years?
> How do I rid myself of my life-long negative beliefs and
> doubts that creep in?

The desire for answers led us to design our own personalized plan in order to transform our lives. We wanted a tool to guide us. Our task was clear: to put together an interactive workbook addressing all our questions; creating exercises and techniques that would enable us to incorporate *The Secret* into our daily lives.

The next step seemed logical. Share this workbook with others who also had questions and were seeking ways to embrace the principles of the Law of Attraction into their lives on a daily basis. Expansion soon followed. We wanted it to be even more. We wanted it to be an all-encompassing workbook, guide, tool, journal, and resource all rolled up in one, to reinforce, validate, clarify, track, and personalize one's journey. We wanted a book that anyone and everyone could customize into his or her own personal experience. *Living The Secret Everyday: My Secret Workbook* was born.

LEARNING TO LIVE *The Secret*

To live *The Secret* everyday, you must learn to apply the principles of the Law of Attraction. The only way to learn this is to *do* it. You must conscientiously practice it daily. You've heard the old adage *practice makes perfect*. It's never been truer.

Learning theory is clear. There is really only one way to learn how to do something and that is by *doing* it. If you wanted to learn to dance, you dance. If you wanted to learn how to do a new job, you do the job. If you wanted to learn to write, you practice writing – and so on and so on. Reading a book or simply listening to a how-to lecture is not enough to become proficient. Noted psychologist William Glasser tells us that we learn and retain:

> 10% of what we read
> 20% of what we hear
> 30% of what we see
> 50% of what we see and hear

70% of what we discuss with others
80% of what we personally experience
95% of what we teach

Therefore, learning to live *The Secret* everyday with the goal of making it part of your life requires active participation or at a minimum a personal experience with it. We call this learning by *doing* or *engaged* learning. The most powerful models of instruction are interactive; they are the ones where the learner actually participates. This is the foundation upon which *My Secret Workbook* has been designed. It is an interactive experience in which the reader learns by *doing*. It is your tool to live the life you want. With this workbook you will deliberately create and allow yourself to have that world. Step-by-step, *My Secret Workbook* guides you on how to live and *do* what you need to do to have that life of joyful abundance. All the recipes and ingredients for your joyful life are here. All you have to do is start cooking.

USING MY SECRET WORKBOOK

To utilize *My Secret Workbook* most effectively, it is recommended that you begin by reading the workbook in its entirety at least once. Once you have digested all the important principles and the various recipes designed to guide you on your journey to living it everyday, begin.

My Secret Workbook is meant to serve as a guide and action tool, a way for you to incorporate *The Secret* into your life. It is our hope that this practical workbook be your starting point that enables you to design your own life plan or course of action to lead you to the life you want. The purpose of the workbook is to stimulate and inspire you and thereby create an opportunity to examine all the ways you can open yourself up to *The Secret* and the life you want.

Part One is designed to get you started as it reviews summarily the substance of *The Secret* and offers ways to commit consciously to its philosophy. In Part Two, recipes are offered to help you discern exactly what you personally want or desire in your life, while Part Three focuses on how to build faith and belief in these desires. Part Four explains how action is inspired in order to be, do or have what you want. After asking for and believing that you can have all that you want, the only step left is to allow yourself to have it. Part Five offers recipes to cleanse yourself of any resistance that may be preventing you from attaining your desires. Part Six puts it all together with daily activities and menus aimed at inviting into your life experience all that you so choose. Part Seven is all about tracking your journey and recording your personal growth and discoveries.

There is no one way to practice or live *The Secret*. The way you go about doing it is your choice. To this end we have included a series of recipes and techniques, many more than you will need. Choose those recipes that you are attracted to, that you feel you will enjoy doing. Each of you is different and only you know which techniques will benefit you. Make some up. If you get bored with one method, choose another to get energized. You are your own guide; you have a barometer inside you (in the form of your feelings). Listen to it. Trust it.

Using this guide is meant to be fun so don't take it too seriously. Play with it! If it stops being fun or interesting to you, set it aside for a while and do something else. Come back to it when you feel like it.

It is our wish that this book serves as a roadmap to help you explore where to start and take you to where you want to go. We hope that it connects all the dots for you and brings you further clarity of understanding in the application of *The Secret* so that you may deliberately live the life of joyful well-being that you were meant to.

PART I

GETTING STARTED

Getting started on your journey is about waking up your mind so you can create a life of joy and fulfillment. It's about making up your mind to be happy. It begins with a thorough knowledge and understanding of the power of thought and the Law of Attraction.

The good news is that if you are reading these words, you have been attracted to *The Secret* and the information regarding the nature of the most powerful law in the universe. You have already gotten started by being in possession of this workbook.

Part One presents a summary of the principles of *The Secret* and stresses the importance of belief in the powerful Law of Attraction. Both understanding and belief are essential to attract what you want into your life. Once you clearly understand and believe its message, *The Secret* will seem like the natural way to live your life. It will be your guide on your journey as you travel from wherever you are to wherever you want to be.

UNDERSTANDING
The Secret

Whatever your mind can conceive and believe, it can achieve.

– Napoleon Hill

WHAT IS *The Secret?*

According to the best-selling book *The Secret*, the secret of life is the Law of Attraction. However, *The Secret* is not alone in purporting this theory. This is not a new idea nor is *The Secret* the first best-seller that has broached this subject. The Law of Attraction has been the focus of many treatises and best-selling books for close to a hundred years. From the early 1900s, beginning with Wallace Wattles (*The Science of Getting Rich, 1910)* and James Allen (*As A Man Thinketh, 1912),* to Napoleon Hill in 1937 *(Think and Grow Rich)* and Esther and Jerry Hicks, pioneering the teachings of Abraham since the 1980s *(The Law of Attraction, 2006),* we've heard about the effect of the power of thought and the Law of Attraction on our lives. In fact, Napoleon Hill coined the term *The Secret* as early as 1937 in his book.

Basically, the Law of Attraction says, *that which is like unto itself, is drawn.* In other words, like attracts like. This is the most powerful law in the universe that affects all things, including thoughts.

According to the Law of Attraction, that which you focus on, think about, believe, and expect will come into your life. Your power is in your thoughts.

To be, do, or have what you want you must think or focus upon what you want. *See* what you want. *Believe* you can have what you want. Your thoughts are like magnets that bring to you the same things that you focus on. These magnetic thoughts attract to you the resources, the people, the things, inspired actions, and circumstances of life that reflect what you are thinking about.

The basic premise is what you think about comes to you. Those magnetic thoughts attract the same; both good and bad whether you like it or not. If you want a life of joy, you must think joyfully. But be careful. If you think negatively, you may get a life of hardship. For example, by continually focusing on being broke or poor, you will never get rich because you are worrying about or thinking about the lack of money in your life. According to the Law of Attraction you will attract more of the same, more bills, more financial issues, more lack of money. Instead, if you want to attract money, you must focus on wealth. Use your thoughts or imagination to make believe you already have the money. See it in your life. As you do this, you will feel better about money and as you feel better about it, more will come into your life. Think wealth and wealth will come.

Your thoughts are powerful things when mixed with a clear and definite goal, persistence, and strong desire. The choice is yours. You create your own reality with your thoughts. You allow that which you want into your experience either deliberately or by default. It can be a wonderful reality or a miserable and unhappy reality. You can focus or think deliberately about what makes you happy or you can by default look at *what is* and think about and wallow in all the problems and conflicts you face in your life.

Whichever you choose, you will get more of the same. Whatever you think about will come to you. Only you are responsible for your life.

Remember, too, that only you have control of your thoughts. Nothing happens in your life unless you invite it in through thought. You choose what to allow into your mind by focusing on it. In essence, your feelings serve as a guidance system, telling you whether you are thinking positively or negatively. You choose to feel good or bad by virtue of what you allow yourself to focus on or think about. If you focus continually on thoughts like lack of money, you feel bad. However, if you focus on and appreciate what you do have in life, what you are thankful for and what you want, you feel good. And remember, the Law of Attraction will attract more of the same. The power of your positive thinking is amazing.

Clearly then, looking at what you want and what you appreciate is more productive than looking at *what is*. But beware of the influence of others, yourself, and your environment. They can block you from getting what you want. Most of us are trained early on to focus on problems, fears, doubts, and listen to others that discourage us. Once you realize this is the wrong road to take, you can deliberately and consciously *stop, delete, and cancel* these negative influences and program your mind with happy thoughts. After all, you cannot control others and they cannot control you. People cannot make you feel bad unless you choose to focus on or think about them and what they have said or done. People cannot enter your life or experience unless you allow them into your thoughts by paying attention to them. It is up to you to decide whether you are going "to beat the drum" by thinking over and over about a critical comment a friend made to you or whether to move on and let it go. Similarly, a circumstance that you observe or participate in cannot be part of your experience or reality unless you invite it into your thoughts. When you look at the world, you can choose to focus on the good things or the bad things going on. You can sift through *what is* for the positive or negative. You can see a world torn by war for or see a beautiful beginning to unfold as people demand peace. You can see the glass half-full instead of half-empty.

WHY DOES *The Secret* OR LAW OF ATTRACTION WORK?

You come into this world in what appears to be a solid human body but actually you are just energy in human form. You are pure, positive energy, meant to live a life of joyous well-being …to be, do, and have whatever you want. A key to understanding *The Secret* is understanding the *full you.* You are more than the "you" we see. Yes, you are a physical human body in this physical world, but that's not all. There is also the non-physical part of you, called your spiritual side, your soul, your inner being – whatever you want to call it – that you cannot see. An understanding of the both parts of you and their relationship is essential to comprehend who you are. When you connect the two through the power of positive thought, you are complete. Your positive thoughts and feelings bring you into alignment with who you really are and opens your world to limitless opportunity. Those positive thoughts allow you to manifest in your life what you want because of the Law of Attraction.

Unfortunately, as you grow up in this physical world, you are shaped and influenced by the environment and people that teach you bad habits of negative thinking and expectations. Too often you are taught to focus on *what is* and what you don't want rather than what you do want; to focus on the problems rather than what's right in your life. Consequently, if you do not live deliberately and consciously concentrating on the positive, you live by default; on auto-pilot according to your negative ideas and thoughts you were trained to think. Life becomes a struggle. A pattern develops. The Law of Attraction brings you more of the same.

The good news is that at any point in time you can make a decision to change your life by changing your thoughts and beliefs. When you change your thoughts, you change your life. When you change the way you look at the world, the world changes for you. When you are thinking positively, you move toward *You* – the non-physical you, the inner you, the joyful you. Your feelings tell you whether you are moving in the right direction. They are your guidance system. When you feel good, you are allowing yourself to connect to who you really are – the joyful happy you; when you feel bad you are resisting that connection. When you pay attention to your feelings (that are produced by the thoughts you encourage and choose) you know if you are "going with the flow'" toward a life of joyful well-being where everything you want will be attracted to you; or if you are fighting the flow by going upstream toward a life of struggle.

Everyday is a new beginning – if you choose to make the best of it. Wherever you are is fine; you can get to wherever you want to be from there. Just make up your mind to be happy.

TAKE THREE STEPS: *ASK, BELIEVE, AND RECEIVE*

When you truly understand and accept that the Law of Attraction will manifest in your life limitless opportunity for happiness and abundance, you are ready to attract *all that you want*…all that you are meant to have. Your only task is to use your power of thought to connect to that positive and loving spirit inside of you. Then all you have to do is: *Ask, Believe, and Receive.* Ask for what you truly want and desire in life. Believe and expect that you can have it. Create that picture in your mind that it is already yours. The

Law of Attraction will respond and you will receive whatever you desire.

The Secret
IN A NUTSHELL

A Personal Declaration

To effectively live *The Secret,* you must have faith in the principles of the Law of Attraction. You need to believe that you can be a powerful creator and that by virtue of your own power of thought, you can create your own reality. You must convince yourself that you are responsible for your own life. This is an incredibly empowering feeling necessary to achieve all that you want in your life.

Declare to yourself out loud or in writing everyday these important principles below. Memorize them. Make them part of the necessary working equipment of your mind because the more you believe, the more powerful you become. Put this mantra on an index card and say it daily at least two times to yourself early on.

Recipe 1: Personal Declaration

I am a powerful creator.

I can be, do, and have anything I want.

All I have to do is choose those positive thoughts that make me feel good.

I focus on what I want, what I appreciate, what I am thankful for.

My feelings will guide me to create positive thoughts and release all negativity from my mind.

These positive thoughts will bring more positive thoughts, experiences, and people into my life, transforming my desires into my physical reality.

In essence, this means that you *must* do, say, and think things that make you feel good. When you do this, you deliberately create the life you want rather than live a life by default. You actively create the life you desire rather than allow life to simply happen to you. By taking control of your mind, you can deliberately or consciously decide to think, act, and speak positively about things that make you feel good. You can *stop, cancel, and delete* those negative thoughts that make you feel bad. Your feelings tell you when you are on the right track. When your thoughts create feelings of happiness, hope, passion, excitement or joy, you empower yourself. You feel, "I can be, do and have whatever I want." However, when you allow negativity to enter your mind then that anger, fear, frustration, and depression block "you" from receiving that life of joyous abundance. You feel the discord, the disconnection. And remember, the Law of Attraction is bringing you more of the same. So pay attention to how you feel. Let go of those negative ideas, beliefs, and influences and make room for the positive thoughts to bring you the life you want.

THE MAGIC
OF BELIEVING

Believe It Can Work For You!

Believing is truly the magical component behind *The Secret*. It is so essential that you believe *The Secret* can work for you in order to successfully make your journey to that life filled with all your dreams. You've heard the wise proverb: *If you think you can, you can. If you think you can't, you can't.* It's never been said any better than that. You must believe that you can create the life that you want. For what you believe forms the framework for the life you create.

The stronger and more deeply felt your faith in the Law of Attraction and your belief that it can work for you, the more successful you will be. Affirming daily your faith in the process will strengthen your belief and thereby empower you to be, do or have all that you want.

Here are two recipes to develop your faith in the process and affirm and strengthen your belief in the principles of the Law of Attraction. The first recipe can be found in the last section. Read and say it daily (and eventually memorize it).

1. Read (and eventually memorize) the *Personal Declaration* in Section Two of this part every evening and during the day when you remember until you are thoroughly convinced that it will accomplish for you all that you want.
2. Still lacking a bit of self-confidence in your ability to have it work for you? Try this affirmation below for ten minutes a day. Taken from *Think and Grow Rich* by Napoleon Hill (slightly modified), it is a five-step affirmation to build and strengthen your faith and belief.

Recipe 2: Self-Confidence Affirmation

1. *I know that I have the ability to achieve the object of my definite purpose in life; therefore, I demand of myself persistent, continuous action toward its attainment, and I here and now promise to render such action.*
2. *I realize the dominating thoughts of my mind will eventually reproduce themselves in outward, physical action, and gradually transform themselves into physical reality. Therefore, I will concentrate my thoughts for thirty minutes daily upon the task of thinking of the person I intend to become, thereby creating in my mind a clear mental picture.*
3. *I know through the principle of autosuggestion (creative visualization) any desire that I persistently hold in my mind will eventually seek expression through some practical means of attaining the object in back of it. Therefore, I will devote ten minutes daily to demanding of myself the development of self-confidence.*
4. *I have clearly written down a description of my definite chief aim in life, and I will never stop trying until I shall have developed sufficient self-confidence for its attainment.*

5. *I fully realize that no wealth or position can long endure, unless built upon truth and justice; therefore, I will engage in no transaction which does not benefit all whom it affects. I will succeed by attracting to myself the forces I wish to use, and the cooperation of other people. I will induce others to serve me, because of my willingness to serve others. I will eliminate hatred, envy, jealousy, selfishness, and cynicism, by developing love for all humanity, because I know that a negative attitude toward others can never bring me success. I will cause others to believe in me, and in myself. I will sign my name to this formula, commit it to memory, and repeat it aloud once a day, with full faith that it will gradually influence my thoughts and actions so that I will become a self-reliant and successful person.*

GETTING STARTED
Ingredients at a Glance

• Read the message of *The Secret* as many times as you need to in order to develop a thorough understanding of what it is and why it works.
  ~Your understanding will only strengthen your belief and desire to keep you living it everyday.

• Develop faith in the fact that the Law of Attraction will work for you.
  ~Say and write the *Personal Declaration* daily.
  ~Affirm to yourself that you *can* do it.

• Develop confidence in yourself that you can change your life when you *ask, believe,* and *receive.*

PART II

ASK

If You Want It, Just Ask!

According to the most powerful law in the universe, the Law of Attraction, if you want it, just ask! Yes, it can be as simple as that. Here's why. Whatever you want or desire, think about most, have a deep-rooted belief in, and see unfold in your mind constitutes your dominate thoughts. These thoughts vibrate into the universe by virtue of your asking and focusing on them. The Law of Attraction tells us that what you focus your attention on or think about will be reflected back to you with more *like* thoughts and experiences. The law is responding to your thoughts regardless of what they may be, positive or negative, and attracting more of the same into your experience. In essence, your thoughts (about what you want) act like magnets, reproducing themselves in your life as circumstances, experiences, and things that mirror them.

Sounds simple enough, right? On second thought, it may be a little more complicated. Just figuring out what you really want may be the trickiest part for some of us. And yet without knowing what you want, you cannot create the life that you want. You are missing the blueprint. *Asking* has to be the first step to successfully creating a life of joyful well-being. When you develop a burning desire for something that you really want, it usually ignites powerful feelings so that the vibration becomes much stronger, which in turn will manifest itself that much sooner in your life.

Determining exactly what you want, and how to ask for it, along with setting goals, is the subject of this next part of the workbook. Since what you really *want* is at the heart of *The Secret,* aim to place a clear and definite desire or goal in your thoughts in order for the Law of Attraction to respond. How you ask for what you want becomes critical to attracting what you want. Unless you consciously frame what you want into a positive statement, your thoughts may be inviting into your life things that you don't want. A clear blueprint of your desires is always a precursor to what is to come so here is an opportunity to have some fun designing one.

Remember, to have it, you need to first want it. Then just *ask!*

WHAT DO YOU REALLY WANT?

The starting point of all creation and achievement in life is a definiteness of purpose or stated another way, the knowledge of what you want and a desire to have it. Until you can conceive in thought that which you really want, there can be no fulfillment of your desires. For when you create anything in your life, you always see it first in your thoughts. The idea or thought is like a blueprint. It creates an image of its manifestation, which then magnetically by virtue of the Law of Attraction flows into your personal experience. The thought or idea always comes before the actual manifestation. *I think I'll write a book about how to apply The Secret,* is the thought that preceded the creation of this book. *I need new clothes for my trip,* is the idea that comes before I go shopping and make my purchases. *Lobster for dinner sounds great,* precedes my cooking of a lobster dinner.

The key here is mind control; deliberately using your mind to focus on what you really want. Nature has blessed humankind with total power and control over one thing and that is *thoughts*. You can either control your thoughts or let them control you. You have a choice. You can allow those negative thoughts and beliefs (that most of us have been trained for so long to think about and focus on) to automatically and unconsciously consume your thinking. You can pay attention to your problems and the lack of things and limitations in your life. Alternatively, you can keep your mind busy with thoughts of your own choosing. You can consciously control your thoughts (tapping into that power in all of us) and deliberately put out into the universe all the desires you really want.

Here is an opportunity in the recipes that follow to determine what you really want. Put your desires out into the universe so that they may be reflected back to you. Have fun!

Recipe 3: Brainstorm Your Desires

Sit down in a quiet place where you will not be disturbed with a favorite pen and this workbook. Close your eyes and ask yourself, "If I had a genie's lamp in front of me and I could wish for whatever I wanted, what would I wish for?" As the thoughts flow into your mind, write them on the chart entitled *Brainstorm/My Prioritized List* on pages 22 and 23. Then prioritize them in terms of importance by placing numbers one through ten next to each entry (with one being the most desired). Now rewrite your list in order of importance on the chart. Enough space is left for you to come back at a later time to add to the list as you discover more desires within you.

Recipe 3: Brainstorm Your Desires

BRAINSTORM	MY PRIORITIZED LIST
1.	1.
2.	2.
3.	3.
4.	4.
5.	5.
6.	6.
7.	7.
8.	8.
9.	9.
10.	10.

Recipe 3: Brainstorm Your Desires

BRAINSTORM	MY PRIORITIZED LIST
1.	1.
2.	2.
3.	3.
4.	4.
5.	5.
6.	6.
7.	7.
8.	8.
9.	9.
10.	10.

Recipe 4: Discover and Record Your Desires

An alternative approach for discovering and recording your desires is to organize what you want around specific areas of your life. Again, select a quiet place to compose your lists where you will not be disturbed. On pages 25 and 26, there is a chart divided into five columns with the headings: *Health, Body, Prosperity, Personal Growth, and Relationships.* Think about each area of your life and write down what comes to mind when you ask yourself, "What do I want in each area of my life?" Underneath the chart are some examples of things that you could include under each of the five categories. Pick from the list or add your own. Most importantly have fun as you discover what you want.

Recipe 4: Discover and Record Your Desires

DISCOVER AND RECORD YOUR DESIRES

Health and Body	Wealth	Work	Personal Growth	Relationships

Examples:

I want $10,000

I want to get along with my x

I want to tighten up my body

I want to be health

I want to return to my college weight

I want to feel happy

I want to relax and enjoy life more

I want to redecorate my home

I want to be truthful in all I do

I want to give to friends and family

I want to make more money

I want to be more giving

I want a new car

I want to love my body

I want to be nice to all

I want to be a good listener

Recipe 4: Discover and Record Your Desires

DISCOVER AND RECORD YOUR DESIRES

Health and Body	Wealth	Work	Personal Growth	Relationships

Recipe 5: Intensify Your Desires

Select your top three to five choices of things that you most desire. It's up to you as to how many you select. When just getting started, one or two may be sufficient to concentrate on. Next, ask yourself, "Why do I want each of these things?" Your answers will strengthen or lessen your desire for them. Record your responses on the chart: *Intensify Your Desires* on pages 28 and 29. Look at your list daily, read it, think about it, and add or change it as you choose. Ask for these things in your mind or read the list out loud focusing on the words.

Recipe 5: Intensify Your Desires

INTENSIFY YOUR DESIRES

1. I want

because

2. I want

because

3. I want

because

Recipe 5: Intensify Your Desires

INTENSIFY YOUR DESIRES

1. I want   because

2. I want   because

3. I want   because

MY BLUEPRINT

A Vision Board

A fun and constructive way to begin living *The Secret* is to create a personal blueprint. Define those things, elements, experiences, and relationships that you want to bring into your life on a vision board. It is a great way to begin building that new life, remembering that no matter where you are, you can always get to where you want to be. After all, you wouldn't build a house without a set of blueprints, so why would you create your life without one?

Most people think about *what is*. Their thoughts are responding to what they are observing, often the problems they are facing or the lack of what they have rather than looking at the limitless opportunities in front of them. They are not creatively controlling their thoughts. Instead they are allowing their thoughts to control them. When you make this vision board you can deliberately and creatively envision positive thoughts of what you want, exercising complete control to attract into your life what you want. The finished product is a daily reminder of what to focus on.

A vision board is usually a collage of images. A beautiful sample of one is on our cover. If you are artistic it can be done in just about anyway, through the medium of a drawing, painting, or a combination thereof. It depicts pictures of things you desire to be or have in your life. It is a valuable opportunity to take an inventory of what you want in your life, a chance to form a clear, sharp vision of everything you want to invite into your personal experience. It is a great tool to reflect on and discover your desires. As you look through newspapers, magazines, catalogues, etc. new ideas of what you want will be born. Have fun!

Recipe 6: Build Your Blueprint

Build your vision of the life you want in three steps:

1. Gather magazines, brochures, photographs, books, cards, lettering, catalogues, and newspapers or surf the Internet to search out images or words that depict all the things you want to invite into your life experience. Print from the Internet and or cut out pictures of those things that exemplify what you want. Include pictures of homes, clothing, cars, jewelry, travel destinations, images of physical attributes, photos of people together reflecting relationships, lottery tickets, checks, bank statements, etc. The key is to select images that represent what you desire.

2. Purchase a piece of oak tag or styrofoam board (any dimension you like) and glue your clippings on to it, making sure to include a picture of yourself in the center. You may add drawings or paint directly on it. Organize your images in any way you'd like. Be creative. Remember, you are the creator. This is your vision and blueprint for your life. Have fun!

3. Place it on a wall, dresser or wherever you will see it on a daily basis. Spend a few minutes everyday looking at it and thinking about it. Take in your new life as you have designed it and feel good that it is on its way.

BE CAREFUL WHAT YOU ASK FOR

How to Ask?

How you *ask* for what you want is critical to attracting what you want into your life. Framing your desires in your mind correctly can make all the difference between getting what you want and getting what you don't want. "Be careful what you ask for" takes on a whole new meaning here. The more you understand the power of the Law of Attraction, the more you realize the importance of deliberately directing your thoughts and couching them in positive statements.

Sometimes your deep-rooted patterns of negative thinking block you from framing what you want constructively. When asked, "What do you want?" your response can be destructive and bring into your experience what you don't want. Instead of responding with desires, you may be stating what you don't want. Saying I don't want to be poor; I don't want to be fat; I hate my job, etc. focuses you on poverty, on being overweight, and hating your job rather than on thinking prosperity, health and fitness, and a successful career.

The recipe below will help you to discover the things you want by showing you how to frame them so your focus is on what you want rather than what you don't want. Remember, the Law of Attraction will bring to you a mirror image of your thoughts, whether you want them or not. So be careful of what you are asking for and how you ask.

Recipe 7: I Know What I Don't Want- A Place to Start

For those of you having a hard time determining exactly what it is you want, listing what you *don't* want may be good place to start. Sometimes it's easier to see those things you don't want because you are so used to couching things in the negative. However, this is a technique that may lead you to discover what you do want since the opposite of what you *don't* want may be the positive way of stating exactly what it is you do want. Try it.

On the next page is the chart entitled *I Know What I Don't Want*. Write a list of the things that you don't want in the first column. After you have written that list, restate each statement as a positive statement under the second column labeled *What I Do Want*. A couple of sample entries are provided.

Recipe 7: I Know What I Don't Want – A Place to Start

I KNOW WHAT I DON'T WANT - A PLACE TO START

WHAT I DON'T WANT	WHAT I DO WANT
I don't want to be fat!	*I want to be slim.* *I want to weigh 124 pounds.*
I hate my job.	*I'd love to find a job in sales.* *I'd like to be a teacher.*

Recipe 7: I Know What I Don't Want – A Place to Start

I KNOW WHAT I DON'T WANT - A PLACE TO START

WHAT I DON'T WANT	WHAT I DO WANT

7

SETTING GOALS

To Discover What You Want

Setting goals is a technique to use to discover what you really want in life. Goals should be both short-term and long-term. Begin with simple daily goals. Then set goals by the week, month, and year. As you set goals, keep in mind that they should be fluid. Goals can change and change often. They are not "set in cement" but be sure you truly want them so that you persevere in your attainment of them. The goals you select are meant to give you direction and serve as a focus for your creative energy. They should help you to achieve your purpose. Most of all, goal setting is meant to be an enjoyable process that should be both expansive and enlightening. The goals you select should make you feel good; both uplifted and challenged at the same time.

There are some *do's and don'ts* you should be aware of before beginning the process of goal setting. When a goal is not accomplished, do acknowledge it to yourself and decide to keep it as a goal or let it go. Don't focus on your failure to reach your goal but rather focus on creating and accomplishing the next one. Do pat yourself on the back when you accomplish a goal. Be proud of yourself, feel that positive feeling of accomplishment. Don't overwhelm yourself by setting too many goals. The fewer the number of goals you have set, the stronger the focus you can maintain on each one. Let your feelings be your guide. Don't set goals that are unrealistic; goals that you know cannot be reached. It's very important to *believe* your goals are attainable. When you set goals you see as unreachable, it's easier to give up and rationalize that you'll never reach them anyway. Choose goals that you genuinely want. The more you want a goal, the more power behind it and the more likely you will persevere to reach it.

Recipe 8: Setting Short-Term and Long-Term Goals

The purpose of this recipe is to give you practice in setting goals, help you discover what you want, and show you that what you want can become a reality. Start the process of setting goals with simple short-term goals. A short-term goal is a goal that you intend to accomplish in a day, a week or even a month, while a long-term goal could take a year to five years to reach. In the chart that follows on the next page record some short-term and long-term goals that you believe you can achieve. Start out by picking simple goals around work, money, relationships, leisure activities, personal growth, etc. As you accomplish a goal, mark an "x" under the column "done" and pat yourself on the back.

Recipe 8: Setting Short-Term and Long-Term Goals

SETTING SHORT-TERM AND LONG-TERM GOALS

Daily	Week	Month	Year	Goal	Target Date	Done
			X	To get a new car	Jun. 2008	X

Recipe 8: Setting Short-Term and Long-Term Goals

SETTING SHORT-TERM AND LONG-TERM GOALS

Daily	Week	Month	Year	Goals	Target Date	Done
			X	To get a new car	Jun. 2008	X

ASK
Ingredients at a Glance

- Develop a clear vision of what you want for that joyful life.
~Build your vision on lists, charts, vision boards or by setting goals as described in the recipes. Select those recipes that appeal to you.
~Place visual reminders of your desires wherever you will see them daily.

- *Ask* for what you want.
~Frame you desires so you are focusing *positively* on what you want. Remember the Law of Attraction will bring you a mirror image of your thoughts and words.

- Strengthen Your Desires.
~Ask yourself "Why do I want this?" The stronger the desire- the stronger the vibration you send into the Universe -which the Law of Attraction will respond to.

PART III

BELIEVE

If You Can See It, You Can Believe It!

Believing is the cornerstone of *The Secret* or the Law of Attraction. In order to attract what you want into your life you must believe. The visualization of and belief in what you desire is the second step in the formula.

It is important to clearly understand how the mind operates in terms of what and how a belief is formed and the part the Law of Attraction plays, to comprehend the role of belief in the total scheme of things. Our powerful minds consist of two parts: a conscious mind where all conscious thought and reasoning takes place and a subconscious part, the seat of action, which acts upon our thoughts. The subconscious mind is influenced by the thoughts that you permit to remain in the conscious mind. It is your conscious mind that communicates what it observes, through our five senses, to the subconscious mind. It is the conscious mind that communicates your thoughts, feelings, and beliefs to your subconscious mind. You can therefore deliberately control your subconscious mind by feeding it with thoughts from your conscious mind that you choose to think. It is important to realize that the subconscious mind accepts and treats both real conditions (what we observe with our five senses) and mentally imagined conditions as reality. It does not know the difference. This is why such processes as affirmations and creative visualization (which will be described later in this part) are so powerful in energizing your thoughts to create strong beliefs.

A belief is a state of mind that you may deliberately create by repeated instructions, directions or affirmations fed to your sub-conscious mind. By intentionally making these kinds of sugges-tions to your subconscious mind, you can control what you feed to your subconscious on thoughts of a creative nature. Therefore, you may convince your subconscious that you in fact believe you will receive that which you *ask* for and it will *act* upon that belief and follow up with inspired action in the form of ideas and/or plans. Faith or belief is what gives life, power, and action to the impulse of thought. It is the element that transforms an ordinary vibration of thought into a powerful magnetic force, which then attracts other similar thoughts, ideas, and circumstances to you.

If you understand that a belief is simply a thought that is thought over and over and over again, then concentrating repeatedly on what you want as if you already have it will ignite strong positive feelings associated with having achieved it. It is the combination of belief and the strong feeling associated with having it that energiz-es that vibration so that the Law of Attraction reflects back similar things and situations into your experience. Repeatedly seeing that brand new car in your possession and feeling excited, proud, and happy as if you are driving it *now* is what will inspire action which will eventually bring it to you.

But be careful here. In the same manner, if you focus and wor-ry repeatedly about problems in your life, your life becomes that problem. You could just as well energize the vibration of a thought,

I can't pay my bills and I'll never have enough money, such that you are inviting more poverty into your life. Remember, if the Law of Attraction is about attracting what you want, your thoughts, beliefs, and feelings are the magnets that attract that which you focus on and feed to your subconscious mind. In a nutshell, if you think about what you want, *believe* it, and feel it, it will be yours.

Put in a scientific way, quantum physics tells us that all of the physical universe is energy, including ourselves. We are energy projected into our human bodies that vibrate into the universe. All energy is magnetic; that is, like energy attracts like energy. Our emotions, beliefs, and thoughts are energy we constantly project into the universe; the source of what and whom we attract. If you are depressed, that's what you project into the universe and thus attract people and situations that are depressing. It's about matching energies.

This part of the workbook addresses the *believing* part of the formula and shows you how you can begin to believe that you can really have what you want so that you can invite it into your life. In the recipes that follow, you will learn how to use affirmations, creatively visualize, meditate, and control your thoughts so that you believe and feel that you can have that life of joyous well-being and abundance.

THE IMPORTANCE
OF RELAXATION

Relaxation means releasing all concern and tension and letting the natural order of life flow through one's being.

– Donald Curtis

Relaxation is a state of mind and body. When you are deeply relaxed in both body and mind, your brain wave pattern changes and slows down, allowing you to stop thoughts, clear your mind, and eliminate resistance. It allows the flow of joyful energy to stream through you. Because of this, relaxation is a perfect exercise to do when you first begin creative visualization, an important process described in the next section. You are opening the door for your imagination to create mental pictures. A relaxation exercise for a few minutes daily sets the stage for a successful creative visualization exercise.

Outlined below are the steps for both breathing and relaxation exercises. Begin by doing the breathing exercise and then continue to the relaxation exercise if time permits. After practicing these for a while, they will mesh together and you will find yourself quickly proceeding from one to another.

Recipe 9: Breathing Exercise

This recipe can be done at anytime during the day, at home, or at work. You may do it for five minutes or for fifteen minutes. Whichever you have time for, it will serve as a refreshing break from the day's events. The steps are:

1. Sit in a comfortable chair or lie down, as long as you won't fall asleep.
2. If possible, wear loose clothes and take your shoes off.
3. Close your eyes. Breathe slowly and deeply, inhaling through your nose. Fill up your diaphragm completely. Stop and hold the breath for the count of five. Then slowly exhale the breath through your nose. Take approximately ten breaths per minute.
4. Concentrate on each breath you take and release. Feel it and track it with your mind as you fill up your entire body and then as it slowly leaves your body. As thoughts enter your mind – and they will – let them go. Return to your focus on your breathing.

Recipe 10: Relaxation Exercise

1. Begin your relaxation exercise by starting with a short version of the breathing exercise described above for two minutes. This relaxes both body and mind, setting the stage for your creative visualization.
2. Keeping your eyes closed, begin relaxing each part of your body, one part at a time. Start with your feet and work through each area of your body, as you tighten and then relax each part:

- Take a deep breath as you count to five. Press on your heels, raising the balls of your feet. Hold this for another count of five. Release your breath and relax your feet.
- Take a deep breath as you count to five. Tighten your legs, kneecaps, and thighs. Hold this for another count of five. Slowly release your breath as you relax your legs, kneecaps, and thighs.
- Take a deep breath as you count to five. Tighten your stomach muscles. Hold this for another count of five. Slowly release your breath as you relax your stomach muscles.
- Continue to do the same as you tense and tighten your fingers, arms, shoulders, neck, and each part of your face (squeezing your eyes shut, puckering your lips, making a broad smile and then relaxing them).

3. Feel your body totally relaxed; limp and so heavy you can't lift any part of it. When you try to lift a part of your body it doesn't move. Stay this way as long as you are comfortable with it. Begin your creative visualization whenever you are ready.

Being relaxed feels good! True relaxation is the absence of stress. What you are doing here is stopping your thoughts, and clearing your mind. You may continue to relax even more deeply by creatively visualizing relaxing experiences. Think of a time when you were very relaxed, not a care in the world. You can be lounging on a beautiful tropical beach or just about doing anything you love to do. Visualize it in your mind with enough detail to bring back the way you felt when you were actually there. Feel the sun beating down on you. Feel the sand under you. You will get better with practice. It may take up to two to three weeks of daily practice to feel proficient at it. The more you practice, the easier it becomes and the deeper the relaxation stage you will reach. More details on using creative visualization to create and strengthen your beliefs appear in the next chapter.

Breathing and relaxation exercises can be used several times for different purposes. When you feel negative energy within you, use the breathing exercise to shift your focus from doubts or worry to your breathing. It is also recommended that you do these exercises in the morning upon awakening and at night before going to bed. Your mind and body are most relaxed at these times and therefore receptive. You can do them for a short period of time or for however long you'd like. They can be practiced anytime and anywhere. However, try to select a quiet place and comfortable position whether it is lying in bed or sitting in a comfortable chair.

CREATE IT IN YOUR MIND

Creative Visualization

Creative visualization is a powerful tool to create and strengthen *beliefs*. It is part of the second component of the *Ask, Believe,* and *Receive* formula. It is a technique that uses the imagination to attract what you want in your life. It involves the process of taking an idea or a thought of something you want to bring into your life and imagining it happening *now* as clearly and realistically as possible to manifest your deepest desires. When you combine concentration and feelings with these thoughts, creative visualization becomes a strong, creative, and powerful force vibrating your images into the universe to bring changes into your life.

Creative visualization serves several purposes. It helps you to:

- Create a life of joy and abundance
- Clarify your desires through imagery
- Get rid of negative thoughts
- Relieve stress and tension
- Problem solve by looking at solutions

It is a well-known fact that if you tell yourself something over and over and over again, you can begin to believe it as true, whether it is true or not. Consequently, a man repeating a lie to himself enough may eventually believe it to be the truth. Similarly, thoughts that you deliberately place in your mind and creatively visualize as happening *now* can be powerful. Once magnetized with emotion these thoughts attract other similar thoughts that harmonize with them.

Most of us use our power of creative visualization everyday, often in an unconscious way, without even being aware of it. We plan and conduct ourselves according to the images that move into and out of our minds. Basically we are creating a vision or picture of how we want our life to be in our mind. It is so effective because our mind cannot tell the difference from an imagined event and the real thing. They are treated equally.

Visualization of your desires combined with the associated feelings activates your subconscious mind, which in turn sharpens your intuitive skills, bringing useful ideas to inspire and motivate you to action regarding your desires and goals. Think about your thought or desire as the blueprint and the feelings associated with it as the "energizer bunny" providing the necessary "electricity." Now you can use creative visualization to transform your energy of what you want into a powerful magnetic force to attract the things you want. If you concentrate and feel the associated feelings, this imagery becomes a creative force that makes things happen.

Recipe 11: Creative Visualization

There are four steps involved in creative visualization:

1. *Decide what you want* and set a goal. Do you want a car?

Do you want a better job? Is there something you want to change about yourself? You may want to begin with the simplest goals; those you believe can happen sooner rather than later. You can then work up to more complex and difficult ones.

2. *Create a detailed picture* or image of exactly what you want in your mind. Visualize what you want or what you wish to be. It can be a situation, an object, a relationship or about anything that you desire. You can build any scene you want. Look upon the images or scenes you create in your mind as real; as happening in the present moment not in the future. See yourself in action. Imagine that you already received whatever you desire so the subconscious mind accepts it as fact. If you have to confront an unpleasant or difficult situation, visualize handling the matter easily. See yourself living in the house or apartment of your dreams. See people having dinner there. Create scenes that are alive, colorful, interesting, and real. Visualize friends and family congratulating or complimenting you on your achievement. The more details you incorporate in your vision, the more real it becomes.

3. *Energize your goal with positive feelings.* Build images in your mind that ignite positive emotions. Be moved by what you visualize. Feel the feelings that are attached to what you want. Thoughts and feelings must be connected. As you see the new blue Jaguar parked in your driveway, smile, feel the joy and excitement of having it. Enjoy the creative visualization experience. Have fun with it. If negative thoughts, doubts or fears creep in, shift your thoughts back. This tool will take time to perfect. With time you will master this technique. The more you do it, the better you get at it as your ability to concentrate improves. The key is to persevere. Keep at it.

4. *Repeatedly focus on it.* Once you've got the picture in your head, think of it often. Try to do the visualization for ten minutes at least two times daily, in the morning and evening. If you remember, think about the image a few times throughout the day as well. Each time, you are energizing this image and sending that positive energy out into the universe.

Here are some tips, recommendations and information to consider:

- Begin your creative visualization with a brief two to three-minute meditative/relaxation exercise (see pages 50 and 51). This stops thought, clearing the mind to make room for the visualization.
- Often you may not see a mental picture at first but rather just feel it by imagining you are looking at it. This works just as well. The imagination works differently for each individual. If this happens don't let it worry you. Practice does make perfect. You may practice simply visualizing by picturing things you see and do in your everyday life like brushing your teeth, walking through a park, or having a conversation with a friend.
- To use creative visualization, you don't have to believe in the metaphysical or spiritual ideas.
- Creative visualization should not be confused with daydreaming.
- Creative visualization *cannot* be used to control the behavior of others or make them do something against their will. You are only your own creator of your own experiences. You cannot create for another.

Below are some samples to illustrate how you might approach creative visualization. Here are a variety of different creative visualizations one might build around the desire to lose weight:

1. I see myself getting on the scale. On my scale my ideal weight is registering in black digital numbers – 140 pounds.
2. I see myself running on the treadmill working up a sweat. I feel great.
3. I see myself shopping, finding, and trying on beautiful outfits. They all fit well and look great. I am so happy. I'm now a size 8.
4. I see myself going out with friends and they ask me how much weight I've lost. They tell me how good I look.
5. I see myself going out to dinner with friends and family more frequently. I no longer struggle with myself as to what to order. I am ordering the healthy foods because I have taken control and I can do it. I see myself selecting salmon as my entrée with vegetables and leaving behind the cake. I tell myself "you will be happy if you eat right," and I make this a dominant thought.
6. I see myself on vacation at a beach resort. I am wearing a bathing suit and I am happy with the way it fits. I am enjoying myself.
7. I am empowered. My faith and belief are so strong that they guide me in my weight loss program. I am following this program with such ease. My mind and body know what to do. However, I do remind myself everyday and keep those thoughts going out to the universe.

Recipe 12: Build Your Own Visualization

Select a goal for yourself and creatively visualize it as happening now. Build different scenarios that you can use during your visualization. Write them below. This is a great way to prepare ahead of time and move your creative visualization along more easily and quickly.

1. _____
2. _____
3. _____
4. _____
5. _____
6. _____
7. _____
8. _____
9. _____
10. _____
11. _____
12. _____
13. _____
14. _____
15. _____

THE POWER OF AFFIRMATIONS

Just as relaxation is a powerful tool used in conjunction with creative visualization, so too are affirmations. Affirmations are any positive statements that affirm that something is already happening *now*. They can be spoken silently in your mind, out loud or written. They can deal with physical, emotional, mental or spiritual issues. They can be very general or very specific. They should always be stated in the present tense. Here are a few examples of affirmations:

> *I am happy.*
> *I like my job because it is challenging.*
> *I am eating healthy.*
> *I am a calm person.*
> *I love my life.*

You can use affirmations by themselves or as part of your creative visualization to manifest your desires. The function of an affirmation is literally to transform your thoughts, ideas, and feelings into your physical reality with the end result that you live the life you want. They are meant to replace those negative thoughts with positive thoughts; break the old habits and thereby create new ones.

The reason affirmations are effective is because the subconscious mind cannot differentiate between actual and symbolic reality. Those thoughts (affirmations) repeatedly fed to your conscious mind over and over again are accepted as real. Therefore when you create affirmations, you strengthen beliefs that you can be, do or have what you want. The more you focus on your affirmation or creative visualization, the stronger the belief and feeling behind it becomes. The Law of Attraction responds by matching it and making it your objective reality.

Choose and construct your affirmations carefully. Start simple by beginning with things you believe are within your grasp. Understand that it does take time for changes to manifest themselves.

Here are some tips and recommendations for constructing and using affirmations:

1. Always construct affirmations in the present tense.
2. Phrase affirmations in short and simple sentences. Use positive language only.
3. Use affirmations in creative visualization to make them even more real to you.
4. Add positive emotion to your affirmations. Ask yourself how you feel as you embrace this positive statement. Feel the feeling flow through you. The emotion will make the affirmation more commanding.

5. It is important that you see, say or write your affirmations daily and *regularly*. Be creative: on the scale put a post-it note with the weight you desire; tape a lottery ticket on a wall with the numbers circled or simply sit down and write your affirmation fifty times.

6. As you say and read your affirmations, focus on their meaning so as to increase your belief in them.

Recipe 13: My Affirmation List

Reflect on the changes you want to bring into your life. What do you really want? Write down the affirmation on the list below in a short, simple sentence using positive language. You may use affirmations listed at the end of this section or make up your own. If it helps, you can start by substituting some of your negative thoughts with positive affirmations. For example, for the words, "I am fat" use the affirmation, "I am eating healthy" or "I am at my ideal weight."

1. _____
2. _____
3. _____
4. _____
5. _____
6. _____
7. _____
8. _____
9. _____
10. _____
11. _____

12. _____

13. _____

14. _____

15. _____

Recipe 14: See and Say My Affirmations Regularly

Place reminders, in the form of notes or post-its containing your affirmations, around your home (on your nightstand, scale, refrigerator, bathroom mirror) in your car, or in your office. Focus on the meaning of each word and the message several times a day. See it and say it to yourself in your mind or out loud. The more you practice, the more receptive your mind will be.

Recipe 15: Affirmations to Affirm Me

Focus on your own beauty and strengths as you write affirmations to build confidence in yourself and become the person you want to become. Break the habit of focusing on what's wrong with you. Make a list below. Here is a sampling of four affirmations:

> *I am a hard worker.*
> *I am a giving person.*
> *I am a patient person.*
> *I am a good listener.*

1. _____

2. _____

3. _____

4. _____

5. _____

6. _____
7. _____
8. _____
9. _____
10. _____
11. _____
12. _____
13. _____
14. _____
· 15. _____

Recipe 16: Tape Your Affirmations

Make a tape or CD of your most important affirmations. Play it at bedtime before you go to sleep. Play it in your car as you drive to work. Play it as you exercise in the gym. Here is a sampling of several affirmations. Draw from them or create your own. Write your own below.

I am beautiful.
I have reached my ideal weight, 135 pounds.
I am a giving person.
I love my body.
I am grateful for my beautiful home and all its furnishings.
I am on a healthy weight loss program.
I am grateful for my daughter who brings me so much joy.
I am happy with my life.
Everything is working the way I want it to.
I am writing this book that is being published next week.
My health is perfect and my body knows what to do to maintain this.

My relationship with my ex-husband gets better everyday.
I accept all the monies I have now.
Everything I need is within me.
I communicate with others in a calm and gentle way.
I have everything I want.
My book is on best-seller lists.
I have plenty of time for everything
The more I have, the happier I am to give.
I am healthy.
I am exercising regularly to keep my fit body.
I am vacationing every six weeks.
I have a beautiful forty-foot boat.
I am a patient person.

1. _____
2. _____
3. _____
4. _____
5. _____
6. _____
7. _____
8. _____
9. _____
10. _____
11. _____
12. _____
13. _____
14. _____
15. _____

BELIEVE
Ingredients at a Glance

- You must visualize what you want and *believe* you have it *now* to invite it into your life.

- Relaxation and breathing exercises clear you mind to prepare you for creative visualization. If time allows, try to do at least 2-5 minutes of these exercises.

- Creative visualization is the tool to use to see and create the life you want.
  ~Do it daily and often for at least 10 minutes to believe that you can have what you want *now*.

- Affirmations should be used repeatedly throughout the day. Keep your thoughts focused on what you want to strengthen your belief and your desire. Say them, read them and /or listen to them.

PART IV

ACTION

Your Thoughts Inspire Action

According to *The Secret*, your job is to be a powerful creator to think positive thoughts that will create the reality you want. Those very thoughts that you put out into the universe not only reflect back more of the same thoughts; but snowball until all the necessary resources, including people, ideas, and plans, come into your experience to manifest your desires. Action is key. You must walk in the direction of what you want. You must work on *you*, grow and practice positive thinking daily. Your mind doesn't know the difference between a real action and a symbolic action. So, if you focus on positive thoughts, such as doing something daily that feels good, you will be inspired to take the right action. You will be compelled to do things to create what you want.

Exactly how you will receive that one million dollars, or the new car or the weight loss you are asking for will come to you from the universe by virtue of the Law of Attraction. Yes, the universe will take those thoughts and inspire action within you.

DESIGNING AN
ACTION PLAN

Your thoughts inspire action, action that is natural and effort-less, without struggle. This is because you are acting to receive. You are "going with the flow." The universe is bringing to you what you want through the action inspired within you. When you are ready to receive, opportunities will appear; an impulse to act will emerge from within. Trust your instincts. It is the universe inspiring you. Follow these instincts and feelings to do something. You must trust, believe, and have faith that the universe will respond. Keep your vision clearly in your mind and the action part will come. You need only to see and believe where you are going; the universe will show you how to get there.

The universe is helping you to design your action plan as long as you ask, believe, and are ready to receive. Remember, creating begins in the form of a strong desire. Once your desire is aligned with faith and belief, it vibrates into the universe. The universe responds, sending matching ideas. It is your imagination, the work-shop of the mind, where the action plan for its transition from abstract to concrete is created. Here your desire is given shape, form, and action. Your imagination is the place that designs your action plan. In short, it is your very thoughts that inspire action by appealing to the imagination. Allow your imagination to become the workshop to design your action plan. With your desire in mind, ask for guidance. Chances are the thought has already inspired action on your part.

MAKING CHOICES

Are You Ready?

Getting ready to receive what you want involves making choices to change how you think. You are already two-thirds of the way there if you are reading this section and practicing the recipes up to this point. Once you choose to ask for and believe that you can have what you want and know that you already have it, the universe, by virtue of the Law of Attraction, will bring it to you as long as you are ready to receive.

Think of your life as happening simultaneously on three levels *being, doing,* and *having.* You must *be,* first. You must be who you are; that powerful creator thinking positive thoughts that make you happy *now.* The Law of Attraction will inspire action within you so you do what you need to do to get what you want. However, unfortunately, too often we live our lives thinking that things and people outside of ourselves will bring us happiness. So we engage in a lot of "doing" – working hard and struggling to have what we think will make us happy. We believe that if we work hard, we can get what we want. Then we can be happy. But it is just the opposite. Happiness must begin inside of you. Being happy first allows you to do and have what you want. Choose to be happy *now* by appreciating and being thankful for what you have and everything you want will flow into your life.

All you have to do is make a choice. You can choose to live your life deliberately; a life of joy, well-being, and happiness by taking control of your mind. Alternatively, you can live by default by allowing life to happen to you and your mind to control you. Below is a checklist to measure whether you are making the right choices. Are you ready to receive what you want? Can you answer *yes* to all of these questions?

- Do you choose desires you really want and are clear about? The strongest desires lead to strong beliefs that in turn create strong vibrations that the universe will respond to.
- Do you choose to believe that these desires are yours now?
- Do you choose to throw out any negative influences from yourself and others? Do you refuse to doubt, be fearful of, and follow those old beliefs that hold you back?
- Do you choose to consciously and deliberately be positive and accept where you are? Your feelings will guide you. You must feel good to attract what you want.
- Do you choose to take the necessary action to receive what you want?
- Do you practice daily creative visualization and affirmations? Remember, with repetition your belief, and therefore your vibration, becomes more powerful.
- Do you watch for opportunities or impulses to act on your desires in the form of inspired action coming from the universe?

If any of your answers are *no,* re-evaluate whether you are ready to receive. What area(s) do you need to continue to work on? Continue to Part V to work on allowing yourself to *receive.*

PERSISTENCE

Don't Give Up!

I missed more than 9,000 shots in my career. I've lost almost 300 games. Twenty-six times I've been trusted to take the game winning shot and missed. I've failed over and over and over again in my life. And that is why I succeed.

– Michael Jordan

Persistence is an essential component in your journey to receive that which you want. It is that sustaining of effort to reach your goal despite opposition. It is a state of mind which does not recognize failure. It is that power that enables you to fight in the face of discouragement. When obstacles appear, persistence keeps you from giving up.

History has shown us that persistence is a quality possessed by many great men and women. No matter how many times they were defeated, they eventually found their way to the finish line. Yet one of the major causes of failure, lack of persistence, seems to be common in the majority of people. Most of us are likely to give up when faced with opposition or obstacles. You must be persistent if you want to get what you want. The good news is you can build your persistence by strengthening your desires and beliefs.

Recipe 17: Strengthen Your Desire

Persistence is definitely tied to the power of your desires. A person with a powerful desire will generally persist until he or she attains what he or she wants while a weak desire usually produces weak results. If you really aren't strong in your desire to be, do or have something, you will fail before you start. After all, it is quite easy to give up on something that isn't *really* wanted. Similarly, if you don't believe you can have it, it's difficult to be persistent.

To strengthen your desires, go back to Part II in the workbook and review what you are asking for. Ask yourself, "Do I really want this in my life? Am I willing to face obstacles, challenges, and opposition and still pursue my goal?" If the answer to these questions is *yes*, then keep reminding yourself when faced with a challenge, "I don't fail until I give up. This defeat is only temporary. I am sustaining my effort to reach my desire." If your answer is *no* to either question then re-examine your list of desires. Rewrite your list if necessary.

Recipe 18: Strengthen Your Belief

The stronger you believe you can have something, the more powerful your vibration into the universe will be. If you are riddled with doubts and believe that it is not possible, it will not come to you. To strengthen your belief, go back to Part I of the workbook and continue to practice the *Self-Confidence Formula*. Also, consider practicing more often your creative visualizations and affirmations to strengthen your belief that this desire *is* yours *now*.

YOUR THOUGHTS INSPIRE ACTION
Ingredients at a Glance

- Focusing on positive thoughts will inspire you to take the right action. Change how you think and the Law of Attraction will respond to those changes

- Choose now to *act* deliberately to live the life you want – saying, doing and thinking those things that make you happy.

- Act *now* to live your life deliberately: a life of joy, well-being and happiness by taking control of your mind.
  ~Focus on what you want, what you appreciate, what you are thankful for.
  ~Release all negative thoughts from your mind.

- You must be persistent if you want to get what you want. Don't give up! You build persistence when you really want something and truly believe you can have it. Follow those recipes that help you strengthen those desires and beliefs.

PART V

RECEIVE

Allow Yourself to "Go With The Flow!"

Receiving is about allowing yourself to do, be or have whatever you want. The key word is *allowing*. Basically it refers to "going with the flow" of that beautiful stream of well-being that is inside all of us. After all, you and everyone else are meant to live a joyful life of abundance. It is the natural state of things for you if you "go with the flow."

This is the most fun part of the process: allowing yourself to receive all that you want in life. Yet, at the same time, it is usually, at first, the most difficult to achieve as you seek to get out of your own way. This is because most people are not taught to be positive. Yet being positive is the foundation of this new life you are creating.

If you *allow* things into your life by matching thoughts and energies, the more positive you will be; the more you bring into your life experience that which you want. It is the Law of Attraction, and it happens when you bask in the pleasures of where you are; when you are grateful for the life you have; when you appreciate and *praise* yourself and others; and when you focus on and dramatize what you want and like. It means *not* paying attention to what you don't want and downplaying the negative feelings by not talking or thinking about them and sifting through *what is* to find the positive. It's about clearing out the negative thoughts to make room for the positive thoughts.

Unfortunately, most of us have grown up and been taught to focus on *what is* rather than on what we want. We have been trained to give our attention to the lack of, limitation, difficulties, and problems life hands us. Consequently we struggle against ourselves and the very things we want in life. The only thing preventing us from receiving is our own resistance, in the form of those thoughts we focus on. We need to overcome those blockages: the old beliefs and attitudes, and the repressed emotions of fear, guilt, and anger that stand in our way.

You must live in the present and not the past or the future. You have to let go of the old. You must focus on the positive in your life *now* and accept where you are. The recipes are simple: meditate to clear your mind; let go of old negative thoughts, beliefs, and feelings; be grateful for where you are; appreciate yourself and others and feel the joy of giving. *Allow* your feelings to guide you. And all that you want will be yours.

MEDITATE TO CLEAR
YOUR MIND

Meditating is the time to quiet your conscious mind. It is the time to simply relax, refresh, and rejuvenate by detaching yourself from conscious thought. Most importantly it is also the time to allow you to prepare your mind for creative visualization. A short meditation for fifteen minutes each day can serve all of these three purposes. It can put you in the receiving mode when you use it to shift away from negative thoughts. You may do a simple breathing meditation or combine it with a relaxation exercise. Both recipes are once again repeated below because they are so important to the entire process of living *The Secret*.

Recipe 9: Breathing Exercise

This exercise can be done at anytime during the day: at home or at work. You may do it for two minutes or for fifteen minutes, whichever you have time for. It will serve as a refreshing break from the day's events or as a way to shift away from negative thinking when needed. The steps are:

1. Sit in a comfortable chair or lie down, as long as you don't fall asleep.
2. If possible, wear loose clothes and take your shoes off.
3. Close your eyes. Breathe slowly and deeply, inhaling through your nose to the count of five. Fill up your diaphragm completely. Stop and hold the breath for the count of five. Then slowly exhale the breath through your nose. Take approximately ten breaths per minute.
4. Concentrate on each breath you take and release. Feel it and track it with your mind as you fill up your entire body and then as it slowly leaves your body. As thoughts enter your mind – and they will – let them go. Return to your focus on your breathing.

Recipe 10: Relaxation Exercise

1. Begin your relaxation exercise by starting with a short version of the breathing exercise above for two minutes. This relaxes both body and mind, setting the stage for your creative visualization.
2. Keeping your eyes closed, begin relaxing each part of your body, one part at a time. Start with your feet and work through each area of your body, as you tighten and then relax them:
   • Take a deep breath as you count to five. Press on your heels, raising the balls of your feet. Hold this for an-

other count of five. Release your breath and relax your feet.

- Take a deep breath as you count to five. Tighten your legs, kneecaps, and thighs. Hold this for another count of five. Slowly release your breath as you relax your legs, kneecaps, and thighs.
- Take a deep breath as you count to five. Tighten your stomach muscles. Hold this for another count of five. Slowly release your breath as you relax your stomach muscles.
- Continue to do the same as you tense and tighten your fingers, arms, shoulders, neck, and each part of your face (squeezing your eyes shut, puckering your lips, making a broad smile and then relaxing them).

3. Feel your body totally relaxed; limp and so heavy you can't lift any part of it. When you try to lift a part of your body it doesn't move. Stay this way as long as you are comfortable with it. Begin your creative visualization whenever you are ready.

After a long day at work and thoughts about your day are bombarding you, either relaxation or meditation feels amazing. Also, early in the morning is a great opportunity to clear your mind so you can face the day feeling refreshed and prepare to "create your day."

GRATITUDE

Accepting Where You Are to Move On

Gratitude is the key to unlock the door to a fulfilling life. It is crucial to begin your journey by accepting where you are in order to move on to where you want to be and toward all that you want. You need to be genuinely grateful for what you have and where you are in life *now*. It is about being thankful and appreciative for the things in your life *now*. If you accept where you are, you *allow* the feeling of well-being to stream through you. Focusing on what you have that you are grateful for will bring on positive feelings and the ability to get what you want. On the other hand, complaining about not having what you want will bring on negative feelings and exactly what you do not want.

Keep in mind, however, that it doesn't matter where you are; what matters is if you *accept* where you are so you can move on toward a joyful life. Life is about being happy *now*. It's about sifting through *what is* and focusing on all the glorious parts of living *now*. It's not about waiting for things to happen, money to come, pounds to be lost in order to be happy.

Unfortunately, we are raised and trained to believe the opposite; that happiness is a byproduct of our achievements. We believe: if I am successful, I will be happy. If I get the right job, I'll be happy. If I get my beautiful home and car, I'll be happy...and so on and so on and so on. We are taught to look outside ourselves for happiness when the true source of happiness is inside. We focus on what we don't have and struggle to get it. We focus on what we want in the future that simply spotlights what we lack *now*. When we say, "I will be happy when I lose fifty pounds," we put attention on being overweight now. And remember that the Law of Attraction will bring you anything you focus on whether you want it or not. The problem is that too many of us spend our lives promising ourselves that happiness will come, when it's right here now, under our noses.

When we look closer at ourselves, at all the wonderful things and people we have in our lives, we feel happy. We feel good. When we feel good we attract those things we want. We send a positive vibration into the universe to which the Law of Attraction responds. When we feel gratitude for the life experience we are living now, we connect with the joy of living in the present. Oh, how glorious that feeling is! The Law of Attraction then responds by bringing us more and more and more – all that we could ever want.

Recipe 19: My Gratitude List

Make a list below of all the things you are genuinely grateful for in your life. You will be amazed at how long the list will be and how it will expand the more you do this. Keep going. Read your list regularly and pay attention to the good feelings that follow this kind of thinking. Include statements like: I am grateful that I own this cute home; I am grateful that I have a savings account; I am grateful for my beautiful and loving daughter; I am grateful that I have a job that I enjoy doing.

1. _____
2. _____
3. _____
4. _____
5. _____
6. _____
7. _____
8. _____
9. _____
10. _____
11. _____
12. _____
13. _____
14. _____
15. _____

Recipe 20: My Wake-Up Call

Upon rising, take a couple of minutes while remaining in bed to think about and verbalize out loud or in your mind what you are grateful for. You might say things like, "I am grateful that the sun is shining. I am grateful that I work with Carol, a wonderful office manager and colleague. I am grateful that I slept like a baby last night and feel so refreshed." What a positive way to get out of bed each morning and start the day! It feels good. List some ideas below of what you might be grateful for upon rising.

1. _____
2. _____
3. _____
4. _____
5. _____
6. _____
7. _____
8. _____
9. _____
10. _____
11. _____
12. _____
13. _____
14. _____
15. _____

Recipe 21: My Gratitude Post-Its

Take a series of strips of paper or post-its and write on each something you are grateful for from the list above. Post them around the home where they will be constant reminders of all the wonderful things in your life. Read them out loud as you come across them. Include them on the bathroom mirror (read as you brush your teeth); the refrigerator (read before you are about to have your meal); the wardrobe mirror (read as you get dressed); on the dashboard of your car (read as you are about to start the car); on your computer, and wherever else you will see them. Change them every so often if you find yourself tiring of them.

Recipe 22: My Gratitude Shifters

Plan accordingly for those "bumps in the road" on your journey. Use gratitude as a way to shift away from negative feelings and thoughts that pop into your mind and are difficult to let go of. You're worried about a friend who is ill; you had a fight with your husband; you didn't get a birthday card from your sister. Consciously shift by bringing forth a thought of something you are grateful for that makes you feel a bit better, which in turn will bring forth another positive thought and another. Your mind cannot think more than one thought at a time. Stocking it with positive thoughts leaves no room for the negative ones.

Here are a couple of ways that I personally shift: I have a beautiful message I have saved from my daughter on my cell phone. When I feel bad, I play and replay her loving message that moves me on to the right track. Another shifter thought I use is remembering the moment when I crossed the finish line of my first twenty-six-mile marathon and how proud I felt. Record some gratitude shifters you can use below.

1. _____
2. _____
3. _____
4. _____
5. _____
6. _____
7. _____
8. _____
9. _____
10. _____
11. _____
12. _____

13. _____

14. _____

15. _____

Recipe 23: I Am Grateful for This Day

Go about your day *looking* for things to be grateful for and appreciate. Express what you are grateful for out loud or to yourself. Thank or tell others how you appreciate them and what they have done for you. It can be something as simple as: I am grateful for how I was treated at my meeting; I am grateful that traffic was easy today; or I am grateful that I got a parking spot; I appreciate the beautiful job my secretary did on my report; or it could be simply a thank you to someone for listening so well.

Recipe 24: Thank You for My Day

Before you retire at night, take a few minutes before you drift off to sleep to reflect on the events of your day. Focus on the positive things that occurred. State out loud or in your mind those things you are grateful for. What a wonderful way to end your day and begin sleep!

Make a list of those things that took place during a day that you could be grateful for. The more you are able to focus on things you are grateful for, the more grateful you will become.

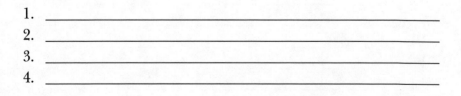

1. _____

2. _____

3. _____

4. _____

5. _____
6. _____
7. _____
8. _____
9. _____
10. _____
11. _____
12. _____
13. _____
14. _____
15. _____

APPRECIATE YOURSELF
AND OTHERS

Appreciation is also a state of mind that will continually bring joy and happiness into your life. Being thankful for what you are, have or done, or thankful to others for their deeds produces a warm, wonderful feeling inside you. It is the positive energy flowing through you out into the universe, only to be matched with more of the same.

APPRECIATE YOURSELF

Appreciating, loving, and caring about yourself are a *must* in order to complete your journey toward getting what you want. Self love and belief in oneself is the source of real empowerment. Empowerment (truly believing that you can be, do or have whatever it is you want in life) is your destination. With the feeling of empowerment comes no greater feeling of joy. That is our natural state of well-being, that joyous stream that flows through all of us. It is only when you block the flow or "paddle" against it with your fears, doubts, and old beliefs that you prevent yourself from getting what you want.

A question often asked is, "If you won't let anyone else put you down, criticize you or make fun of you without getting upset, why do you do it to yourself?" Once again most of us have been raised to see ourselves too often as not worthy or even not likeable. We tell ourselves we're too fat, we're stupid, we haven't accomplished anything in our lives. We beat up on ourselves when we make a mistake. We have been trained to focus on what's wrong with us rather than what's right with us. We are taught to believe that in order to grow and have a successful life we should tear ourselves down and then rebuild by amassing things and accomplishments outside ourselves. If I make two hundred thousand dollars a year, I will prove to myself that I am a "good" person – smart and accomplished. Then I can feel good about me.

But once again we have it in reverse. Your beauty is inside. You need only to find it. You must clear yourself of those old beliefs and make room for the new ones. Your thinking must change. You must focus on all the wonderful qualities that you possess. When you change the way you think about yourself, your whole life will change.

Remember, according to the Law of Attraction, you attract into your life what you think about including what you think you deserve. Your inner thoughts and feelings are projected outward and, like a magnet, attract things, experiences, and people that are in accord with those thoughts and feelings. If you believe you are worthy and value yourself, you will radiate these good feelings about yourself into the universe. It is all about feeling. If you create a good feeling, you can be that positive, powerful creator of your life. You must find more ways to love yourself because once you love yourself you can then love others. Also, keep in mind that the more you appreciate yourself, the better you will feel and the happier you will be. This flow of energy then radiates through you into the universe and the Law of Attraction responds to you, attracting more of the same.

Recipe 25: Who Am I?

Make a list of your positive qualities below. Include your physical characteristics, your personality traits, your talents, your intellect, etc. Get as detailed as you can. Include words and phrases like: beautiful eyes, caring person, energetic, perservering, good writer, honest, good friend, etc. From time to time read and re-read them to reinforce and focus on feeling good about you.

1. _____
2. _____
3. _____
4. _____
5. _____
6. _____
7. _____
8. _____
9. _____
10. _____
11. _____
12. _____
13. _____
14. _____
15. _____

Recipe 26: Treat Yourself Right

Make a list of things you enjoy doing. Include things such as listening to music, meeting a friend for lunch, playing a sport, reading a book, watching a movie, etc. Try to do one or more of these things everyday just to feel good. It is amazing how we forget to treat ourselves to the simple things we so enjoy. Continue to add activities to your list and most of all do them. Some suggested activities are listed here:

- Have fun using your talents and abilities. Do those things you enjoy like playing an instrument, practicing a sport, working on a craft project or writing a poem.
- Spruce up your living accommodations to keep them attractive and comfortable. Display any awards you may have and any pictures of family and friends you cherish.
- Buy yourself a new dress or suit that you feel good in. Dress in clothing you feel you look attractive in and which you find comfortable.
- Spend more time with people who you enjoy and make you feel good about yourself. Avoid those who make you feel uncomfortable or make you feel bad about yourself.

1. _____
2. _____
3. _____
4. _____
5. _____
6. _____
7. _____
8. _____
9. _____

10. _____
11. _____
12. _____
13. _____
14. _____
15. _____

Recipe 27: Catch Up

Do something you have been putting off for a long time. This could include writing a letter, calling a friend, cleaning out a cabinet or a drawer or organizing your closet. The delightful feeling of accomplishment beats out that negative feeling tugging at you when you procrastinate. Make a list to remind yourself.

1. _____
2. _____
3. _____
4. _____
5. _____
6. _____
7. _____
8. _____
9. _____
10. _____
11. _____
12. _____
13. _____
14. _____
15. _____

Recipe 28: Affirm Your Beauty

Turn the positive qualities that you listed in the *Who Am I* recipe into affirmations (see pages 60 and 61 to review how to write them). Select those qualities you admire most about yourself. Write your affirmations below, say them out loud or to yourself anytime. Pay attention to how you feel. A few examples are listed here for you:

> I am intelligent.
> I deserve everything good.
> I am a creative person.
> I am beautiful.

1. _____
2. _____
3. _____
4. _____
5. _____
6. _____
7. _____
8. _____
9. _____
10. _____
11. _____
12. _____
13. _____
14. _____
15. _____

Recipe 29: Visualize the Real You

Use creative visualization to see you the way you want to be. Make a list of those qualities you would like to develop in yourself; what you would like the real you to become. Create a picture of yourself having those qualities...being thin, happy, or healthy. One scenario might include you being complimented for how you look. Another could be you putting on that size 8 pair of pants or seeing yourself happy in a new relationship. You could visualize yourself at the doctor's office and being told you are healthy.

APPRECIATE OTHERS

When you start to truly appreciate yourself and your own beauty within, you will begin to notice that you can't help but appreciate the beauty in others. The more you appreciate others, the more you will find to appreciate in others. The more you appreciate others, the more you will appreciate yourself. It's circular. Focusing on appreciation of others has incredible benefits. When you pay attention to appreciating others and discover their beauty the better you feel. When you genuinely say, "thank you" or "I really appreciate what you did," you feel good. You are on the road moving in the right direction toward what you want. Yes, sometimes others are rude and thoughtless, but you do have a choice. You can focus how mean it was of a friend to miss your birthday or you can focus on all the other birthday parties she attended. You decide. Remember, pay attention to how you feel.

Unfortunately, many of us have not been raised to think like this. Too often we take for granted the good deeds and acts. We pay way too much attention to how we are mistreated. We focus on the negative effects that others have on us. The problem is that by wallowing in pity for ourselves, we take on a victim mentality of having been wronged and feeling bad about it. The Law of Attraction responds with more negative thoughts. Remember our thoughts, negative or positive, are magnets attracting the same. When you do this, you are no longer in a receiving mode but rather resisting or disrupting the flow of the stream of well-being. So consciously put a spotlight on the positive in others, and express your appreciation. The Law of Attraction brings you more of the same.

Recipe 30: Thank You for Being You

Make a list of special people in your life and jot down next to each name what you appreciate about them, admire about them or why you are glad they are in your life.

Example: Andy, thank you for being such a great friend. You are wonderful to be around because you are so upbeat and supportive.

1. _____
2. _____
3. _____
4. _____
5. _____
6. _____
7. _____
8. _____
9. _____
10. _____
11. _____
12. _____
13. _____
14. _____

15. _____

Recipe 31: Express Your Appreciation

Make a phone call, write a letter or an email, give a small gift or simply use your words to say thank you to those "special people" you listed above. You may just want to say "I love you," or "I do so appreciate you being there for me" without a specific act to provoke it. If you admire something about someone, let him or her know. Compliment others. It all feels good!

THE JOY OF GIVING

You've heard the phrase, *the joy of giving*. And chances are you probably have experienced it too; that wonderful, warm, and happy feeling you get when you've given that *perfect* gift or performed an act of kindness or simply gone out of your way to help someone in need.

Giving can take so many forms. It can be a gift, a donation to a charitable cause, an act that benefits others, or an act that provides value and service to the world. It can be a compliment, an expression of love, words of appreciation or a simple smile.

Giving is a great opportunity to experience positive feelings of happiness and joy and by virtue of the Law of Attraction bring more of the same to you. Acts of kindness and caring benefit both the giver and receiver. They produce instant good feelings for both parties as each is lifted into a state of feeling happy. Giving is a chance to feel the positive energy flow through you. You are "going with the flow" toward joy and well-being. Since the universe (including you) has an infinite supply of love and happiness, your acts of giving and sharing only make room for more to come to you. It is the giving that keeps that stream of positive energy flowing to you so you may receive all that you want. Here are some recipes to feel the joy of giving.

Recipe 32: Giving Through Appreciation

Appreciating others in your life, what they do, and who they are is a wonderful way to give to others. It can be done in writing or simply with words directed to friends, colleagues or family members. Use the phone, email, or give a gift. Make sure you give thanks to those who have done things for you. If you admire something about someone, let him or her know with compliments.

Recipe 33: Thank You for My Life

Each morning give thanks for what you have in your life and create that positive stream of energy going out into the universe to bring back more of the same. Start with your grateful list and keep adding to it.

Recipe 34: Share with Others

Share things that you value with others. Give away possessions you have that you do not use anymore. A donation of clothing to the Salvation Army or Goodwill is a good example.

Recipe 35: Charitable Donations

Give a monetary donation no matter how large or small to those in need.

Recipe 36: Splurge on Yourself and Others

Many people are careful about how they spend their money because they have been trained in scarcity and then want to hold on to it. Today, spend a little more money on things you want and don't worry about finding that bargain. Buy your friend lunch or buy that something for yourself that you always wanted (but was being frugal about) to reinforce the belief that there is no limit and that this will come back to you.

LETTING GO

Cleanse and Forgive

In order to receive all that you want, you must feel good *now* about you and your world. You must be grateful for what you have, sift through *what is* to find the positive and appreciate yourself and others. It's time to cleanse yourself of negativity; forgive others, and let go of past events that have negatively influenced you. Release all of it from your thoughts. If you hold on to anger because you can't forgive, you bring more of this negativity into your life. You are only hurting yourself by carrying this old baggage around with you. You can't move on to what you want when you pay attention to what you don't want. Instead you are attracting more negative experiences and people into your life who perpetuate this reality. Every negative thought or feeling is blocking the "good" from coming to you.

The key, then, is to accept where you are now and make peace with it so that you can move on without resistance to what you want. In order to make room for new positive thinking, you must get rid of old beliefs, ideas, and thoughts which keep you in a resistive state; those old thoughts that simply contradict what you want. You must forgive those who have hurt you. When you hold on to the anger and hurt, you get stuck. You keep bringing more and more of the same into your life.

Making peace is about cleansing and forgiving. It is about opening yourself up to allow positive energy to flow. It's about letting go of negative thoughts that are *holding you back* or blocking you from getting what you want. It's about focusing on the positive and:

1. Letting go of any negative doubts and fears that you have been trained to think that don't allow you to be who you really are. It's about not being a victim anymore; not being powerless.
2. Letting go of feeling bad about yourself or unworthy.
3. Letting go of anger and hurt that another has caused you.
4. Letting go of experiences that have negatively affected you.

It's about regaining your power. When you take control of your life, you become that powerful creator of the life you want.

Recipe 37: Forgiveness - My Life in Review

Forgiveness is an amazing tool to let go of patterns of negative thoughts, beliefs, and behaviors. If forgiveness is, "giving up the hope that the past was different and saying thank you for the experience," (Oprah show, February 2007) then forgiving is a wonderfully cleansing approach to set the stage for a life of joy. If you can accept that every experience in your life has made you the person you are then you can not only forgive but even be thankful that you have learned something from it.

Here is a recipe to evaluate yourself and determine if you are holding on to old baggage. Find a quiet place and reflect on your life beginning now and going backwards in time. As you begin to review it, ask yourself questions. Are there people or experiences or events in my life that have had a very negative affect on me and still continue to evoke strong negative feelings in me? Am I angry about someone or something? Are there memories about myself that do not feel good? Once you have found such a memory, let yourself see the image of it. See in your mind what exactly it was about and then forgive yourself or another and be thankful for the experience. An example might be: being fired from a job and hostility carried around as a result.

Recipe 38: Changing your thoughts – Shifters

When you *allow* negative thoughts of worry, doubt or fear to enter your mind, the Law of Attraction aligns with them and more negative thoughts will soon be on their way. It is a "snow-ball effect"; a chain reaction. The answer is to release the negative thoughts as soon as possible. Replace them with positive thoughts since you can't think two different thoughts at the same time. Start to observe the change in your feelings as confirmation that you are changing your thoughts. Any relief felt is a step forward- don't expect to jump from anger to joy. Your feelings are your guidance system to let you know if you are in the positive or negative zone.

Prepare ahead of time to be ready to shift thoughts by making a list of shifters. Write down those thoughts that could quickly change a negative thought and evoke a positive feeling or at least a feeling of relief. Don't expect to go from total frustration to joy instantaneously. But, if you can feel a bit of relief, of hopefulness, you are on your way. This will start the chain reaction of attracting more and more positive thoughts.

When a negative thought enters your mind, let it go. Say to yourself, "I will receive what I choose to think. My feelings will guide me." Then replace the negative thought with a shifter thought. If one doesn't work try another. The key is to refocus and feel the good feeling that attaches to it. Write your list of shifters below. They can be any thought that is uplifting and makes you to feel better. The shifter thought can be: a heart-warming memory, something humorous to make you laugh, something you are really looking forward to, a thought about a person you have loving feelings for, or something you have done that you are really proud of.

1. _____
2. _____
3. _____
4. _____
5. _____
6. _____
7. _____
8. _____
9. _____
10. _____
11. _____
12. _____
13. _____
14. _____
15. _____

Recipe 39: Affirmations to Change Negative Thoughts

Affirmations are a great tool to also change your negative thoughts to positive ones. Use affirmations to cleanse your mind especially when there is a recurring negative thought. For example: when you find yourself frequently putting yourself down because of some mistake you have made, substitute positive affirmations for those thoughts. Say to yourself things like:

> *I do many things well.*
> *I am proud of me.*
> *I am smart.*

Convince yourself of these truths by repeating these affirmations over and over when you are able to.

Recipe 40: Let Go - Stop, Cancel, Restate

You've had a fight with a friend or spouse and some mean words were exchanged. You were mistreated by someone you care about and it hurts and angers you. You are right and someone refuses to hear you. Consequently, these intense angry feelings surface and you can't let go of them. You keep replaying the same scenario over and over again in your mind.

The problem is that the more you think about it, the more you will think about it. As a result, you are in the process of attracting something you do not want; in this case a tense and unhappy relationship. Because your thoughts are so attractive, once you get stuck in that angry feeling that doesn't feel good to you, it's easier to keep focusing on that thought and build up more and more negative energy than to shift to a positive thought.

Instead, a good technique to use is S*top, Cancel, Restate.* It goes like this:

Stop:	Tell yourself: "I am feeling a very negative emotion. I don't want to feel this way."
Cancel:	"I know what I don't want. I don't want to fight with him."
Restate:	"I know what I do want. I want to work it out together." "I want to agree to disagree." "I want to have a harmonious relationship." Alternatively, say to yourself, "I want to feel good."

With those kinds of restatements, your thoughts will start to feel a little better and a little better and a little better as you attract matching thoughts and feelings.

WHEREVER YOU ARE, YOU CAN GET TO WHERE YOU WANT

A Personal Inventory

The road to change involves exploring, discovering, and changing your deepest, most basic attitudes and beliefs about life. In the process you often discover ways in which you have been holding yourself back from achieving a happy, fulfilling life. You discover the fears, doubts, and negative thinking patterns that have held your mind at a "standstill."

Before you can *allow* yourself to "go with the flow," your mind must be prepared to *receive*. You need to protect yourself against all the negative influences, whether they are of your own making, influenced by others or just negative events happening around you. Probably your biggest weakness as a human being is allowing yourself or others to negatively block your journey.

Recipe 41: Personal Growth and Discovery

Below is an inventory of questions, the answering of which can lead to much personal growth and discovery about yourself. The more knowledge and understanding you gain about yourself, the more you will be able to consciously clear out the negative influences, which are blocking you from "going with the flow."

As you read each question, analyze yourself carefully to determine if this is an issue you need to address. Read the questions and state your answers so you are truthful with yourself. Put a checkmark next to each question you need to continue to reflect on. Write about any issues you need to examine in your journal at the end of the workbook. Come back to these questions once a week and do this exercise for few months. You will be amazed at how much you have learned about yourself. Once you recognize that you have the willpower to fight off these negative influences, you are ready to receive.

A Personal Inventory

Do you let others easily influence you against your own judgment?

Are you a complainer and, if so, what are the reasons?

Do things occur that disturb and annoy you but you tolerate them? Why?

Do you have a life goal in mind and, if so, do you have a plan to achieve it?

How do you protect yourself from the negative influences of others?

Do you utilize creative visualization to make your mind positive?

Is there someone in your life that inspires you and why?

Do you criticize other people easily?

Can you state three of your worst qualities? What are you doing to change them?

Are you a magnet for other people's problems?

Do you feel obligated to listen to other people's problems? If so, why?

What can you learn about yourself by looking at the friends that you attract?

Do you complete everything that you start?

Do you change your mind frequently? If so, why?

Are you easily enamored by people's wealth or position in life?

What is your biggest worry? What do you do about it?

Are you worried about what others think?

How important are material possessions to you?

Do you need to use liquor, drugs or cigarettes to reduce your anxiety? If yes, why don't you try willpower instead?

Do you look at your life and future with little hope?

Do you like your job? If not, why?

Does you job inspire you with faith and hope?

What part does religion play in keeping your mind positive?

What things that other people do annoy you most?

Do you use sarcasm frequently in conversation with others?

Do you learn from making mistakes?

Are you jealous of those people who do extremely well?

Do you frequently feel sorry for yourself? If so, why?

Do you sometimes feel total joy and other times have a feeling of hopelessness?

Do other people's weaknesses annoy you? If so, why?

Do you usually see the "worst" in people before the "good?"

Are you careless about your personal appearance?

Are you opinionated and refuse to listen to others?

Are the people you are closest to mentally superior or inferior to you?

Do you purposely avoid relationships with anyone? If so, why?

Do you worry about friends or family? If so, why?

Do you deal directly with your problems or avoid them?

Do you frequently make mistakes in your life? If so, why?

Have you learned anything today? Personal growth? Knowledge?

Do you try to profit from mistakes and failures by analyzing and reflecting on them?

Do you find that you easily annoy other people?

Do you blame others for your unhappiness? If so, why?

Do you have relationships that negatively influence you?

How many hours out of your day do you spend on work, sleep, and play?

Among your relationships, who is most encouraging, most discouraging, and most cautious in their advice?

Are you happy? Why or why not?

What traits about your personality do you like or dislike? Why?

Are you an aggressive or timid person?

What are your deepest fears: poverty, loneliness, sickness, old age, etc.?

Are you a cynical-type person that doubts what others say?

Do you have difficulty receiving criticism? How so?

What do you desire most and what are you doing to get it?

RECEIVE
Ingredients at a Glance

- Receiving is about allowing yourself to "go with the flow" of that stream of well-being inside all of us. It's about feeling good about you and your world.

- Meditate daily for 10 minutes to clear and relax your mind and body, making yourself ready to *receive.*

- Accept where you are *now:*
  ~Express how grateful and appreciative you are.
  ~Sift through *what is* for the positive.
  ~Take time to appreciate yourself and others.

- Do things to feel the *joy of giving* and put yourself in the receiving mode.

- Release negative thoughts – they are only blocking "good" from coming to you.
  ~Use affirmations, shifters and *letting go* recipes.
  ~Forgive and cleanse yourself of old beliefs and feelings- that old baggage that only holds you back.

- Explore and reflect on *who you are.* Above all appreciate yourself. Select and use recipes to make the changes you want for a happy and fulfilling life.

PART VI

PUTTING IT ALL TOGETHER

It's time to put it all together. This part of the workbook reviews and reinforces those important principles and techniques to live your life consciously on a daily basis. First and foremost you must have a thorough understanding of the nature of the most powerful law of the universe and accept that it works. This is your starting point, so let's recap here.

The Law of Attraction tells us that everything that happens to us, whether good or bad, we attract to ourselves. Your thoughts, reflected in what you actually believe, think, say or do are powerful. They generate feelings that in turn attract things, people, and experiences into your lives. You can create the reality you want by deliberately focusing on positive thoughts that generate good feelings. The key is to pay attention to how you feel. Your feelings will guide you. They will tell you if your thoughts are in alignment with what you want so that the Law of Attraction may bring it to you.

Everything in the universe is energy including ourselves. What controls the flow of energy are our thoughts, beliefs, and feelings.

As a vibrational being, you naturally generate thoughts and feelings of love, peace, and abundance unless you are blocking yourself or resisting "going with the flow." The Law of Attraction reflects back to you in an expanded version similar thoughts, experiences and people – either good or bad depending on your thoughts. It is the feelings attached to these thoughts that actually send out a wave into the universe and anything that's vibrating on the same frequency gets attracted into your life. Your task is to align your thoughts, beliefs, and feelings with what you want so you are going in the right direction toward love and joy. Action will then follow, inspired by your thoughts so that you may be, do or have all that you want.

Your greatest power is your ability to control your mind. Yes, you can help thinking the thoughts you do. You can control your thoughts. You can, through willpower, change the nature of your thoughts and even refrain from thinking altogether. All you have to do is consciously be aware of your thoughts, knowing you are a constant creator of your life. Your feelings are the barometer to tell you what you're thinking. When you are thinking harmonious and positive thoughts you feel good. When you are thinking negatively – anxiety, fear, depression – you feel bad.

Therefore, nothing is more important than how you feel. When you are consciously aware of your feelings, you can then choose those thoughts that make you feel good. You can make every moment a time to create the perfect life that you can imagine. That is why learning to embrace the Law of Attraction is a personal opportunity for deep and meaningful growth. You will find your natural state of joyful well-being as you discover and let go of those old beliefs, fears, doubts, and attitudes that have been preventing you from a life of fulfillment.

With this knowledge, let's put it all together. How do you live *The Secret* today and everyday? You must practice those recipes that enable you to be that powerful creator. All it takes is practice; daily practice. The more you practice on a regular basis, the easier it becomes to live that life you want. Start off slowly, be patient, and give yourself time to get proficient. It doesn't happen overnight. Allow yourself to slip up, retreat, and then move forward. Don't beat yourself up when the negative feelings creep into your thoughts – and they will. Be grateful that you are aware of them and move on to where you want to be. In the beginning, it's like learning a new dance: two steps forward, one step backward. Be kind, patient, and loving to yourself. This is the essence of *The Secret.*

BELIEVE YOU CAN CHANGE

Believing you *can* change is crucial. Believing you can be a powerful creator is essential to changing your life. You must believe that you do have a choice, to deliberately create what you want in life or alternatively to create a life by default. You must believe that you do have control of your thoughts, which are the power behind attracting the life you want. You must believe that no matter where you are you can get to where you want to be.

If you believe these principles, you will change. You will begin to be a positive thinker, focusing on what you want consciously and a positive creator attracting what you want into your experience. If your belief needs a bit of strengthening simply return to Part I and continue practicing the recipes to build your confidence in the process and yourself.

CREATE YOUR DAY
EVERYDAY

What you are living today and tomorrow is a result of your thinking. If your thinking changes so too will your life. If you expect great things, great things will come. If you expect bad things, bad things will manifest themselves. Since you can deliberately build the life you want, consider starting step by step by creating each day, everyday, in advance. By positively thinking about your day, you set up a wonderful feeling tone for your day. Focusing on a positive, productive day in advance is a great way to attract the things you want into your life everyday.

Take a few minutes each morning before getting out of bed to paint a picture of your day. *See* it unfolding in your mind, the way you want it to turn out. *Expect* it. When you start expecting things, you are creating. Talk to yourself and see the events happening in your mind. Include such visions as:

> *Traffic is really light today.*
> *I feel really productive here today.*
> *The important conference meeting is going well.*

I enjoy creating with my colleagues.
I eat a healthy lunch.
I complete all my work. I do a great job.

As you see these things, feel the associated feelings. Feel good that each one of these things is happening the way you want it to *now*.

PAY ATTENTION TO
HOW YOU FEEL

As you put together all the principles of the Laws of Attraction you soon realize that nothing is more important than how you feel. How you feel tells you if you are in alignment with *you;* the joyful *you* that can be, do, and have anything you want. Alignment is a prerequisite to inspired action and manifestations that follow. How you feel is an open window into your thoughts. What you feel tells you what you are thinking. Positive thoughts make you feel good. Negative thoughts make you feel bad. Attracting all that you want into your life requires positive thoughts.

In a nutshell, the key to successfully living *The Secret* is deliberately choosing thoughts that make you feel good everyday. Make a point to:

- Look for the positive in *what is.*
- Give praise and appreciate.
- Be thankful for what you have.
- Focus on what you want.
- Think about warm memories.

Throughout your day pay attention to how you feel. Appreciate that you have this barometer called feelings within you to keep you on track. Don't beat yourself up when you think negatively. Appreciate both your positive and negative feelings because they tell you your guidance system is working. Ultimately, they tell where you are in relation to where you want to be. They tell you if you are on course or need to get back on course.

Every emotion you feel lets you know the appropriateness of what you are thinking, speaking or acting. When you are in harmony with your inner being, you are moving in the right direction toward joy. However, when you are not in harmony with what you want, you feel the discord. And whenever you are feeling negative emotion, you are mis-creating either through your thought, your word or actions. You must trust that your guidance system is the most important feedback you will get. Only you know what is good for you.

Too often, though, we don't always trust ourselves. Instead we look to others who we think know more clearly what is good for us. We look to society for rules to tell us what is right and wrong. We lose sight of what's good for us as we overwork ourselves because that is what we are suppose to do to get ahead and be happy. We need to stop that kind of thinking now and follow our hearts. In short, pay attention to how we feel.

We can't say this enough because only you yourself know what is best for you. Is that being selfish? Our answer is yes. And that's okay. You need to be selfish (meaning doing what is best for you) in order to align with your inner being and achieve the life you want. Once you understand that there are no limits, that there is an abundance of everything in the universe and enough for all, you welcome selfishness in this context for everyone.

USE YOUR AFFIRMATIONS
THROUGHOUT THE DAY

Affirmations are powerful tools to put you in a receiving mode. Use them throughout your day to keep you in a positive state-of-mind, to strengthen your beliefs, and to keep you focused on what you want. The more you repeat them and see them as being, the more power you bring to these thoughts and desires.

The human mind is constantly attracting vibrations that harmonize with that which dominates the mind. Any thought, idea, plan or purpose which one holds in one's mind attracts a host of its relatives, adds these 'relatives' to its own force and grows until it becomes the dominating, motivating master of the individual in whose mind it has been housed.

– Napoleon Hill

Aside from saying affirmations to yourself during meditation times, find opportunities to use them throughout your day. Say them to yourself silently (or out loud if you can) and truly focus on the words. See the affirmation as happening *now*. Feel the positive feeling that comes with believing this affirmation. Do this any time during your day, whenever you remember. Say them while you are brushing your teeth, showering, driving to and from work, as you do housework or while you exercise. Recording affirmations on a tape recorder, on your iPod or CD player and listening to them over and over again in the car, at the gym or on a walk is effective. Your recording can be detailed or simple. It can be in the form of a one-sentence affirmation or a total creative visualization of you being, doing or having whatever you want.

Use affirmations in conversation with friends, family, and work colleagues. Use strong, complimentary statements to others about people (and yourself) and things you want to see in a positive way. They should be genuine feelings that you have. The more positively you speak, the more positive and happy you feel.

THE POWER OF MUSIC

PLAN ACCORDINGLY

Music is a powerful tool that can evoke emotions in us that seem to come from nowhere. These emotions have the power to color our moods, affect our thoughts, and change our perceptions of the world as well as generate behavioral patterns. We know that when we feel excited or optimistic, we feel empowered, which in turn inspires and attracts more positive thoughts, ideas, and actions into our world.

Music is an excellent way to put yourself into the "receiving" mode because it can cleanse your mind of resistive negative thoughts and replace them with uplifting feelings that inspire the creation of more of the same.

Recipe 42: *Plan Accordingly* - Music Can Inspire

Plan Accordingly (Arrica Rose and the Dot, Dot, Dots 2006) has been chosen as the theme song for *Living The Secret Everyday: My Secret Workbook* because of its inspiring lyrics that subtly define and encapsulate the exciting journey you are about to take:

Two tickets for the moon,
Got nothing to lose.
A rocket ship to change,
Darling we're on our way.
Take life, as she comes,

Why is she shooting arrows and firing guns?
Well, I heard there's life on Mars,
You've heard I have a heart

Occasionally, the world is an unhappy place,
So, plan accordingly,
Please plan accordingly.

Feels like I've been crying for over 100 years
And there's still no river and way too many tears.
So I say so long to sorrow,
You've been a good friend of mine.
But, for every new beginning,
Something's got to die.

Here we are in a one-room palace,
Tomorrow seems like such a challenge.
Close your eyes, baby, I'll whisper in the dark
Get ready, set, depart.

Occasionally, the world is an unhappy place,
So, plan accordingly,
Please plan accordingly

When you combine these lyrics with its opening, soothing and soulful melody and follow it as it climbs to a crescendo of an ever-increasing volume and upbeat rhythm, feelings of excitement and empowerment are born in its listeners. It is a powerful practice to sit back, close your eyes, listen to (sing along if you like) and focus on the inspiring lyrics, melody, and beat of the song. Feel the feeling of exhilaration and joy that engulfs you at the thought of this journey. It's a time to just "go with the flow." Play the song on your iPod or CD player and listen to it whenever you want to remind yourself of the wonderful journey you are experiencing, erase existing negative thoughts or just transport yourself to a place of positive emotion. You may download the song free on our website www.livingthesecreteveryday.com.

Recipe 43: Deliberately Create Feelings With Music That Touches You

Since all music has an inherent emotion, you can use it to create or recreate emotions in yourself. Music is a personal experience that can produce various emotional responses in different individuals. Consequently, you often hear people say, "This is my song," when a special emotion is associated with it. It may result from the actual nature of the music, its lyrics or melody or because it is associated with a past positive experience in someone's life. For myself, when I listen to and focus on the lyrics and melody of John Lennon's song *Imagine,* I am transported to a peaceful, comforting, and positive place. On my way to work at 6:30 am, I often start my day feeling positively uplifted as I sing to myself the simple chorus of a classic song:

Oh what a beautiful morning,
Oh what a beautiful day,
I have a beautiful feeling,
Everything is going my way.

To use music as an uplifting tool, select those songs that touch your emotions. Go to iTunes for ideas or select from our list below. Download the music from iTunes (to your iPod, computer, or CD player); music that moves you to a positive place. Then focus as you listen to it while getting out of bed in the morning, driving to or from work or as you just simply meditate on it, allowing the music to carry you to wonderful feelings. Below are a few recommended songs that may fit the bill. Add your own list of music below.

Don't Stop Thinking About Tomorrow, Fleetwood Mac
Imagine, John Lennon
I'm a Believer, The Monkees
I Believe I Can Fly, R. Kelly
Silence is All We Need, Arrica Rose

1. _____
2. _____
3. _____
4. _____
5. _____
6. _____
7. _____
8. _____
9. _____
10. _____

11. _____

12. _____

13. _____

14. _____

15. _____

RECIPES FOR LIFE

Menu Planning and Reflection

Living *The Secret* everyday is like baking a fabulous apple pie. The end result of both is your creation; hopefully a scrumptious tasting dessert or a joyful life of abundance. How you get there is dependent on how well you follow the recipes and the exact kind of ingredients you choose to use. Presented in the workbook are over forty recipes to take you step-by-step on your journey. The entire list of *Recipes for Life* appears on pages 139 through 141. Just as you choose between Granny Smith and Macintosh apples for your pie, it's up to you to choose those recipes that appeal to and work for you. There is no one-size-fits-all needed to be successful. Your life experience will be unique to you.

This workbook is designed to give you choices of recipes to select from. We have purposely given you more than what you will need. Your job is to choose one or ten, depending on the amount of time you have. We want you to continue with those that give you a good feeling. Try as many as you like, but continue to use those that affect you in a positive way and make you feel good. Most importantly, have fun.

Early on, use them anytime during the day when you find yourself in a negative place or when you want to be happier. Find out what times in the day certain exercises work better for you. For example: for most people the relaxation and meditation exercises work best in the morning when they awake or at bedtime. However, if your schedule dictates the afternoon, go for it.

Next we have presented five weekly menus; recommending which recipes to follow as you get started. At the beginning, we suggest that you start off slowly and simply. We encourage you to first make your lists of your desires, of what you are grateful for, what you appreciate, and prepare ahead by writing a shifter list. Make the lists short to start because you can and will continue to add to them. We do not want you to overwhelm yourself at the beginning. Soon you will be able to do it all and these exercises will become second nature. It is your life to deliberately create. Good luck!

RECIPES FOR LIFE

PART I GETTING STARTED

Recipe 1: Personal Declaration
Recipe 2: Self-Confidence Affirmations

PART II ASK If You Want It, Just Ask!

Recipe 3: Brainstorm Your Desires
Recipe 4: Discover and Record Your Desires
Recipe 5: Intensify Your Desires
Recipe 6: Build Your Blueprint
Recipe 7: I Know What I Don't Want-
    A Place To Start
Recipe 8: Setting Short-Term and Long-Term Goals

PART III BELIEVE If You Can See It, You Can Believe It!

Recipe 9: Breathing Exercise
Recipe 10: Relaxation Exercise
Recipe 11: Creative Visualization
Recipe 12: Build Your Own Visualization
Recipe 13: My Affirmation List
Recipe 14: See and Say My Affirmations Regularly
Recipe 15: Affirmations to Affirm Me
Recipe 16: Tape Your Affirmations

Recipe 40: Let Go- Stop, Cancel, and Restate

Recipe 41: Personal Growth and Discovery

PART VI PUTTING IT ALL TOGETHER

Recipe 42: *Plan Accordingly*- Music Can Inspire

Recipe 43: Deliberately Create Feelings With Music That Touches You

Menu Planning

On the next few pages are five weeks of sample menus to start living *The Secret* everyday. Recommendations are made as to which recipes to follow each week. But ultimately the choice is yours. Follow the series of sample recipes each week or design your own. Place a check mark before each recipe on the day of the week you have practiced it. Add additional recipes that you have selected to practice each week.

SAMPLE MENUS

FIRST WEEK:_____

Su	M	Tu	W	T	F	S	RECIPES
							RECIPE 1: Personal Declaration
							RECIPE 2: Self-Confidence Affirmations
							RECIPE 3: Brainstorm Your Desires
							RECIPE 4: Discover and Record Your Desires
							RECIPE 5: Intensify Your Desires

SAMPLE MENUS

SECOND WEEK:_____

Su	M	Tu	W	T	F	S	RECIPES
							RECIPE 1: Personal Declaration
							RECIPE 2: Self-Confidence Affirmations
							RECIPE 6: Build Your Blueprint
							RECIPE 7: I know What I Don't Want- A Place to Start
							RECIPE 8: Setting Short-Term and Long-Term Goals
							RECIPE 9: Breathing Exercise
							RECIPE 10: Relaxation Exercise
							RECIPE 11: Creative Visualization

SAMPLE MENUS

THIRD WEEK:_____

Su	M	Tu	W	T	F	S	RECIPES
							RECIPE 1: Personal Declaration
							RECIPE 9: Breathing Exercise
							RECIPE 10: Relaxation Exercise
							RECIPE 11: Creative Visualization
							RECIPE 12: Build Your Own Visualization
							RECIPE 13: My Affirmation List
							RECIPE 14: See and Say Affirmations
							RECIPE 15: Affirmations to Affirm Me
							RECIPE 16: Tape Your Affirmations
							RECIPE 17: Strengthen Your Desires
							RECIPE 18: Strengthen Your Belief

SAMPLE MENUS

FOURTH WEEK: _____

Su	M	Tu	W	T	F	S	RECIPES
							RECIPE 1: Personal Declaration
							RECIPE 9: Breathing Exercise
							RECIPE 10: Relaxation Exercise
							RECIPE 11: Creative Visualization
							RECIPE 19: My Gratitude List
							RECIPE 20: My Wake-Up Call
							RECIPE 21: My Gratitude Post-Its
							REICPE 22: My Gratitude Shifters
							RECIPE 23: I Am Grateful For This Day
							RECIPE 24: Thank You For My Day
							RECIPE 25: Who Am I?
							RECIPE 26: Treat Yourself Right
							RECIPE 27: Catch Up
							RECIPE 28: Affirm Your Beauty
							RECIPE 29: Visualize the Real You
							RECIPE 30: Thank You For Being You
							RECIPE 31: Express Your Appreciation
							RECIPE 32: Giving Through Appreciation
							RECIPE 33: Thank You For My Life

SAMPLE MENUS

FIFTH WEEK:_____

Su	M	Tu	W	T	F	S	RECIPES
							RECIPE 1: Personal Declaration
							RECIPE 9: Breathing Exercise
							RECIPE 10: Relaxation Exercise
							RECIPE 11: Creative Visualization
							RECIPE 34: Share With Others
							RECIPE 35: Charitable Donations
							RECIPE 36: Splurge on Yourself and Others
							RECIPE 37: Forgiveness- My Life In Review
							RECIPE 38: Changing Your Thoughts- Shifters
							RECIPE 39: Use Affirmations to Change Negative Thoughts
							RECIPE 40: Let Go- Stop, Cancel and Restate
							RECIPE 41: Personal Growth and Discovery
							RECIPE 42: *Plan Accordingly*- Music Can Inspire
							RECIPE 43: Deliberately Create Feelings With Music That Touches You

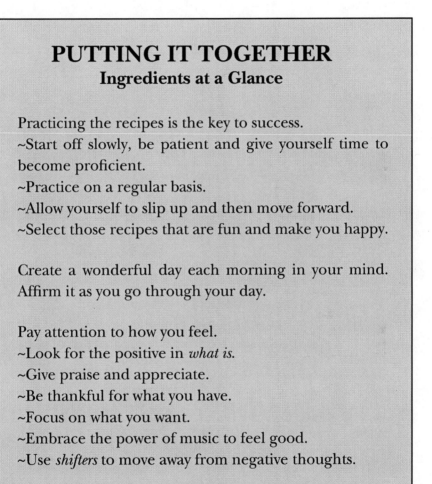

PUTTING IT TOGETHER
Ingredients at a Glance

- Practicing the recipes is the key to success.
  ~Start off slowly, be patient and give yourself time to become proficient.
  ~Practice on a regular basis.
  ~Allow yourself to slip up and then move forward.
  ~Select those recipes that are fun and make you happy.

- Create a wonderful day each morning in your mind. Affirm it as you go through your day.

- Pay attention to how you feel.
  ~Look for the positive in *what is*.
  ~Give praise and appreciate.
  ~Be thankful for what you have.
  ~Focus on what you want.
  ~Embrace the power of music to feel good.
  ~Use *shifters* to move away from negative thoughts.

PART VII

MY JOURNEY

Your journey down the road to a fulfilling life – that path to being, doing, and having all that you want – is one of exciting personal growth and discovery. Your journey is always *now* because your power to affect your life is always in the present. As you define and satisfy your desires and preferences, more and more are born. You never get tired of creating for there is no end to your new desires that flow from you. You continually and deliberately reach to expand yourself when you consciously are aware of how you direct your thoughts and decide that you want to feel good.

The joy of life is the journey. It begins by accepting and appreciating where you are and then moving to where you want to be. Enjoy your journey as you bask in its pleasures: focusing on the positive of *what is*; dramatizing what you want; appreciating and giving praise for what you have. Enjoy this journey as you "go with the flow" and align yourself with that life of joyous well-being. You are in a perfect place to begin your journey no matter where you are or where you want to go. Here is an opportunity to track and record this amazing journey of personal discovery and growth in your journal that follows at the end of the workbook. Enjoy!

TRACKING MY JOURNEY
A Journal

You never know what you will learn till you start writing. Then you discover truths you never knew existed.

– Anita Brookner

Journaling has long been an affective tool to achieving better emotional and mental health. It is a safe tool for self-expression because it is anonymous. It is an opportunity to reflect on where you are and where you want to go as you track your journey. It allows you to map the highs and lows of your journey and look back and remember this emotional and spiritual trip at different points along the way. Along with tracking your emotions, moods, and experiences over time, it is also an opportunity to unburden yourself of old baggage. It's a chance to let go of the hurt, doubts, and fears you inherited as a child and cling to as an adult.

Your journal is a place where you can rain thoughts and ideas from the "crazy" to the sublime. No need to censor your thoughts. They don't have to make sense. It is amazing what you will discover in your journal if you let go and "go with the flow." It is a place to discover, clarify, and achieve your dreams, desires, and goals. Writing down these things is always a first step to realizing them. Personal growth is often the by-product of journaling as it reveals patterns of thought and behavior that can help you as you continue your journey.

Your journal can be all this and more. Have fun and enjoy tracking your journey. Capture your life permanently as you witness your own personal growth and discoveries. Use it to stimulate positive thinking as you make *The Secret* a part of your life. Reinforce its important principles and inspire yourself.

> *To me the greatest pleasure of writing is not what it's about, but the inner music that words make.*
>
> – Truman Capote

27

USING MY JOURNAL FOR PERSONAL GROWTH AND DISCOVERY

Your journal is your tool to track and record the unfolding journey of the creative life about to begin. Use it in any way so that you enjoy it. Watch and record your "road trip" and constantly remind yourself that life is an eternal journey that should always have joyous well-being as its destination.

It is recommended that you make an entry daily, at the end of each day, when you are not too tired to reflect on your day. The length of your entry is totally up to you. Some days it may be a simple paragraph where other days it may be as much as two pages or more. Note that each journal entry page begins with a sentence completion task at the top to get you started. At the bottom of each page is an inspirational quote that could also serve as a starting point (or ending point) as you reflect on what the quote means to you. It is your choice. Approach your journal anyway you want. You may just reflect on your day and record what went well. You may praise, compliment or note your appreciation for yourself and others. You may choose to respond to questions like: How did I feel today? Any new desires spring up? Any self-discoveries or learnings? You may create a vision for tomorrow. Ask yourself if there is anything you want to do: plans, inspired ideas or actions.

Live and record your life as you embrace *The Secret* everyday. Use your journal for personal growth and discovery. What a document to have and look back on in the days ahead! Have fun!

THE ULTIMATE RECIPE

Make Up Your Mind to Be Happy

The ultimate recipe for getting that life of joyful fulfillment can be summed up in six simple words: *Make Up Your Mind to Be Happy*. Three simple steps are its ingredients:

STOP: Trying to find happiness outside yourself by accumulating more things and more money.

START: Being that joyful, happy person inside you *now* – this will inspire you to do what you need to do to have what you want. Focus on loving and appreciating where you are which in turn will inspire you to move toward all you want on this journey called life.

PAY ATTENTION TO HOW YOU FEEL: Consciously and deliberately chase opportunities to be happy now, and all that you want will be yours. It is the Law of Attraction.

May the doors to your life open as you open the doors to your mind.
– Joanne Scaglione and Suzanne Stitz

DATE:	**MY JOURNEY**
NOTES:	*I am thankful for:*

If you mind can conceive and believe, it can achieve.

– Napoleon Hill

_____

_____

_____

_____

_____

_____

_____

_____

_____

_____

_____

_____

DATE:	**MY JOURNEY**
NOTES:	*I am thankful for:*

Be the change you wish to see in the world.

– Gandhi

_____

_____

_____

_____

_____

_____

_____

_____

_____

_____

_____

_____

DATE:	MY JOURNEY
	I am thankful for:
NOTES:	

I am no longer cursed by poverty because I took possession of my own mind, and that mind has yielded me every material thing I want, and much more than I need.

– Andrew Carnegie

DATE:	**MY JOURNEY**
NOTES:	*I am thankful for:*

Every thought of yours is a real thing - a force.
– Prentice Mulford

DATE:	**MY JOURNEY**
	I am thankful for:
NOTES:	

All that man achieves and all that he fails to achieve is the direct result of his own thoughts.

– James Allen

DATE:	**MY JOURNEY**
NOTES:	*I am thankful for:*

_____

_____

_____

_____

To desire is to obtain; to aspire is to achieve.

– James Allen

DATE:	**MY JOURNEY**
	I am thankful for:
NOTES:	

The real secret of power is consciousness of power.
— Charles Haanel

_____

_____

_____

_____

_____

_____

_____

_____

_____

_____

_____

_____

DATE:	**MY JOURNEY**
NOTES:	*I am thankful for:*

If you ask what is the single most important key to longevity, I would have to say it is avoiding worry, stress and tension. And if you didn't ask me, I'd still have to say it.

– George Burns

DATE:	**MY JOURNEY**
NOTES:	*I am thankful for:*

_____

_____

_____

_____

Everyone visualizes whether he knows it or not. Visualizing is the great secret of success.

– Genevieve Behrend

DATE:	**MY JOURNEY**
NOTES:	*I am thankful for:*

Any fact facing us is not as important as our attitude toward it, for that determines our success or failure.

– Norman Vincent Peale

DATE:	**MY JOURNEY**
	I am thankful for:
NOTES:	

The positive thinker sees the invisible, feels the intangible, and achieves the impossible.

– Winston Churchill

DATE:	**MY JOURNEY**
	I am thankful for:
NOTES:	

Discipline is the soul of an army. It makes small numbers formidable, procures success to the weak and esteem to all.

– George Washington

_____

_____

_____

_____

_____

_____

_____

_____

_____

_____

_____

_____

DATE:	**MY JOURNEY**
NOTES:	*I am thankful for:*

Whenever a negative thought concerning your personal power comes to mind, deliberately voice a positive thought to cancel it out.

– Norman Vincent Peale

DATE:	**MY JOURNEY**
NOTes:	*I am thankful for:*

I just hung in there. I never gave up, and I just said, I'm going to make a putt sooner or later.

– Vijay Singh

DATE:	**MY JOURNEY**
	I am thankful for:
NOTES:	

When negative feelings are suppressed positive feelings become suppressed as well, and love dies.

– John Gray

DATE:	**MY JOURNEY**
NOTES:	*I am thankful for:*

_____

_____

_____

_____

Feeling gratitude and not expressing it is like wrapping a present and not giving it.

– William A. Ward

_____

_____

_____

_____

_____

_____

_____

_____

_____

_____

_____

_____

_____

DATE:	**MY JOURNEY**
NOTES:	*I am thankful for:*

The greatest part of our happiness depends on our dispositions, not our circumstances.

– Martha Washington

DATE:	**MY JOURNEY**
NOTES:	*I am thankful for:*

Work joyfully and peacefully, knowing that right thoughts and right efforts will inevitably bring about right results.

– James Allen

_____

_____

_____

_____

_____

_____

_____

_____

_____

_____

_____

_____

DATE:	**MY JOURNEY**
NOTES:	*I am thankful for:*

You can give in to the failure messages and be a bitter deadbeat of excuses. Or you can choose to be happy and positive and excited about life.

– A.L. Williams

DATE:	**MY JOURNEY**
NOTES:	*I am thankful for:*

Big things are expected of us and nothing big ever came of being small.

– Bill Clinton

DATE:	**MY JOURNEY**
NOTES:	*I am thankful for:*

Ask and you will.
– John 16:24

DATE:	**MY JOURNEY**
	I am thankful for:
NOTES:	

When you wholeheartedly adopt a "with all your heart" attitude and go out with the positive principle, you can do incredible things.

– Norman Vincent Peale

DATE:	**MY JOURNEY**
NOTes:	*I am thankful for:*

Develop an attitude of gratitude, and give thanks.
— Brian Tracy

DATE:	**MY JOURNEY**
NOTES:	*I am thankful for:*

As we express our gratitude, we must never forget that the highest appreciation is not to utter words, but to live by them.

– John F. Kennedy

_____

_____

_____

_____

_____

_____

_____

_____

_____

_____

_____

_____

DATE:	**MY JOURNEY**
	I am thankful for:
NOTES:	

_____

_____

_____

_____

Most people are just about as happy as they make up their minds to be.

– Abraham Lincoln

DATE:	MY JOURNEY
NOTES:	*I am thankful for:*

Happiness is when what you think, what you say, and what you do are in harmony.

– Mahatma Gandhi

_____

_____

_____

_____

_____

_____

_____

_____

_____

_____

_____

_____

DATE:	**MY JOURNEY**
NOTES:	*I am thankful for:*

The vision that you glorify in your mind, the ideal that you enthrone in your heart - this you will build your life by, this you will become.

— James Allen

DATE:	**MY JOURNEY**
NOTES:	*I am thankful for:*

I don't know what your destiny will be, but one thing I do know: the only ones among you who will be really happy are those who have sought and found how.

– Albert Schweitzer

DATE:	**MY JOURNEY**
NOTES:	*I am thankful for:*

So many of our dreams at first seem impossible, then they seem improbable, and then when we summon the will, they soon become inevitable.

– Christopher Reeve

DATE:	**MY JOURNEY**
NOTES:	*I am thankful for:*

The best way of removing negativity is to laugh and be joyous.

– David Icke

DATE:	**MY JOURNEY**
	I am thankful for:
NOTES:	

Meditate. Live purely. Be quiet. Do your work with mastery. Like the moon, come out from behind the clouds! Shine.

— Buddha

_____

_____

_____

_____

_____

_____

_____

_____

_____

_____

_____

_____

DATE:	**MY JOURNEY**
NOTES:	*I am thankful for:*

For myself I am an optimist - it does not seem to be much use being anything else.

– Winston Churchill

DATE:	**MY JOURNEY**
	I am thankful for:
NOTES:	

The one without dreams is the one without wings.
– Muhammad Ali

DATE:	**MY JOURNEY**
NOTES:	*I am thankful for:*

Positive thinking can be contagious. Being surrounded by winners helps you develop into a winner.

– Arnold Schwartzenagger

_____

_____

_____

_____

_____

_____

_____

_____

_____

_____

_____

DATE:	**MY JOURNEY**
NOTES:	*I am thankful for:*

The sense of obligation to continue is present in all of us. A duty to strive is the duty of us all. I felt a call to that duty.

– Abraham Lincoln

DATE:	**MY JOURNEY**
NOTES:	*I am thankful for:*

It is done unto you as you believe.
— Jesus

DATE:	**MY JOURNEY**
	I am thankful for:
NOTES:	

Imagination is everything. It is the preview of life's coming attractions.

– Albert Einstein

DATE:	**MY JOURNEY**
	I am thankful for:
NOTES:	

What you resist persists.
– Carl Jung

_____

_____

_____

_____

_____

_____

_____

_____

_____

_____

_____

_____

DATE:	**MY JOURNEY**
NOTES:	*I am thankful for:*

All power is from within and is therefore under our control.

– Robert Collier

DATE:	
	MY JOURNEY
NOTES:	*I am thankful for:*

Follow your bliss and the universe will open doors for you where there were only walls.

– Joseph Campbell

DATE:	**MY JOURNEY**
NOTES:	*I am thankful for:*

You create your own universe as you go along.
— Winston Churchill

DATE:	**MY JOURNEY**
	I am thankful for:
NOTES:	

Many people who order their lives rightly, in all other ways are kept in poverty by their lack of gratitude.

– Wallace Wattles

DATE:	**MY JOURNEY**
NOTES:	*I am thankful for:*

Whether you think you can or you think you can't, either way you are right.

– Henry Ford

DATE:	**MY JOURNEY**
	I am thankful for:
NOTES:	

Let us remember, so far as we can, that every unpleasant thought is a bad thing literally put into the body.

— Prentice Mulford

DATE:	**MY JOURNEY**
NOTES:	*I am thankful for:*

Dream lofty dreams, and as you dream, so shall you become.
— James Allen

_____

_____

_____

_____

_____

_____

_____

_____

_____

_____

_____

_____

DATE:	**MY JOURNEY**
	I am thankful for:
NOTES:	

The secret is the answer to all that has been, all this is and all that will be.
– Ralph Waldo Emerson

_____

_____

_____

_____

_____

_____

_____

_____

_____

_____

_____

_____

DATE:	**MY JOURNEY**
NOTES:	*I am thankful for:*

There's nothing wrong with having your goals really high and try-ing to achieve them. That's the fun part. You may come up short. I've come up short on a lot on my goals, but it's always fun to try and achieve them.

– Tiger Woods

DATE:	**MY JOURNEY**
	I am thankful for:
NOTES:	

What power this is I cannot say. All that I know is that it exists.
— Alexander Graham Bell

DATE:	**MY JOURNEY**
	I am thankful for:
NOTES:	

Whatever we think about and thank about we bring about.

– John Demartini

DATE:	**MY JOURNEY**
	I am thankful for:
NOTES:	

He who cherishes a beautiful vision, a lofty ideal in his heart, will one day realize it.

– James Allen

MY JOURNEY
Ingredients at a Glance

- The joy of life is the journey. Remember your destination is always *now*, not tomorrow. Everyday deliberately reach to bring happiness to yourself by focusing on the positive.

- Track your journey of personal growth and discovery in your journal creating a permanent record to reflect on and stimulate more positive thinking.

- Your journey begins where you are *now*, remembering no matter where you are you can get to wherever you want.

- Make up your mind to be happy, always mindful of the ingredients in the *Ultimate Recipe*.

ABOUT THE AUTHORS

Dr. Joanne Scaglione has been a principal, counselor, and teacher for 30 years. She holds two master degrees in Special Education and Guidance and Counseling and a doctorate in law. She has written and lectured extensively on the issue of raising happy and successful children in the twenty-first century on television, the internet, and at workshops for parents and educators. As a coach and mentor to children, parents and teachers, her philosophy has always been that all children can reach their *limitless* potential with encouragement from us. The key is empowerment. It is only natural that Dr. Scaglione would not only be attracted to the message of *The Secret* but as an educator and counselor want to guide others on how to live *The Secret* everyday. She is coauthor of two children's books: *The Big Squeal: A Wild, True, and Twisted Tail* (2005) and *Life's Little Lessons: An Inch-by-Inch Tale of Success (2006)* as well as the highly-acclaimed parenting book: *Bully-Proofing Children: A Practical, Hands-On Guide to Stop Bullying* (2006), all published by Rowman and Littlefield.

Suzanne Stitz makes her debut as an author in *Living The Secret Everyday: My Secret Workbook,* a collaboration between twin sisters, as she brings a fresh and creative approach based on her own personal experiences with the message of *The Secret*. She is an accountant by profession and excited to be a part of this project. Their journey together has been an exciting one. Her sister, Joanne knew after seeing *The Secret* that she had to share it with Suzanne and quickly recruited her. Together they explored and discovered *how-to* make it a working part of their own lives and find that joyful place inside themselves. The next step was clear- share it with others. *Living The Secret Everyday* was born – a workbook to transform the lives of others as it had and continues to transform their lives. An east coast- west coast duo, Suzanne lives in New York and Joanne lives in Los Angeles. They speak on the phone at least three times a day. They are best friends.